The Power of Gratitude

Rewiring and Rising with Gratitude

KINNARI SONCHHATRA

Qurate
quratebooks.com

The Power of Gratitude
Rewiring and Rising with Gratitude
Kinnari Sonchhatra

Published in 2025

© Published by

Qurate Books Pvt. Ltd.
Goa 403523, India
www.quratebooks.com
Tel: 1800-210-6527, Email: info@quratebooks.com

ISBN: 978-93-58982-57-2

Acknowledgments

Thank you to God, for your loving guidance and the many blessings you have bestowed upon me.

Thank you to my mother and father, Damyanti Thakkar and Vasantlal Thakkar for the code of ethics you taught me.

Thank you to my husband Bhavan Sonchhatra for being the quiet strength behind every word of this book. Your unwavering belief in me, your patience, and your constant encouragement have carried me through moments of doubt and fatigue. Your steady support, gentle reminders, and faith in my purpose made it possible for me to keep going, even on the hard days. To my daughter, Jahnavi Sonchhatra—your love, laughter, and understanding gave me the space and inspiration I needed to create. You reminded me of what truly matters. This book carries a piece of each of you, and for that, I am endlessly grateful.

Thank you to my mentors, Smriti and Dr. Manjunath, for their spiritual guidance and wisdom.

Thank you to my friends for their enthusiasm and support.

My heartfelt thanks to Brejesh Chalill and Sharada S for believing in this work and giving it their voice through their foreword.

Thank you to my publishers Qurate Books and their team.

Mission

To empower people to rise in their life with the magical practice of Gratitude.

In addition, my mission is to donate a percentage of the royalties from each copy of The Power Of Gratitude to non – profit charities including SEENCH India Foundation (www.seenchindia.org) that supports literacy for tribal children.

Foreword

I've had the privilege of knowing Kinnari since we were teenagers—when she already carried the spark of curiosity, compassion, and quiet strength. Over the years, I've watched that spark deepen into something far more profound: the steady glow of a person constantly evolving—first as a thoughtful student, then as a diligent professional and mother, and now as a human being deeply committed to uplifting others.

This book is an extension of that evolution. It is both timely and timeless—a practical guide and a gentle companion. Through it, Kinnari invites us to explore gratitude not as a fleeting emotion, but as a way of rewiring our minds and, through that, our lives. She doesn't preach; she offers. She doesn't claim expertise; she shares experience. That humility is the book's superpower.

One of the most beautiful ideas in these pages is the "ripple effect of gratitude"—the notion that even a small act of sincere appreciation can spread outward, touching others and altering the emotional climate around us. This idea is not only poetic—it's powerful, and backed by science.

Gratitude isn't just a feeling, Kinnari reminds us—it's a practice, a mindset, and a force for personal and collective transformation.

In a world that often rewards urgency over reflection, and accumulation over appreciation, this book is a nudge back to what truly matters. I hope that you finish this book, not just feeling better—but being better.

— Brejesh Chalill

(Brejesh Chalill is a senior leader in Indian banking with over 25 years of experience).

Foreword

One of the easiest ways to express your gratitude to a person for what they mean to you or do for you, is to say Thank You. Similarly one of the easiest ways to apologise to a person for hurting them in any way is to say "Sorry". It sounds easy but it is not so easy to do. Because to do either of them from the heart needs a deep sense of self awareness and an ability to care for the other person and care for yourself too.

I am simply amazed at how sometimes people do not acknowledge others or look the other way after hurting them. And trust me, it's never forgotten.

Kinnari, in this book, gently tugs at you, pokes your awareness making it easier for you to open the door of abundance. The more grateful you are, the more you will have, to be grateful for. She brings in many real life examples that serve as tips to practice the art of gratitude. A tool to enhance the quality and richness of life, of relationships in both professional and personal spaces and more.

Kinnari will make you think deeply and inspire you to become more!

Best wishes
Sharada S

A Letter to My Readers

Dear Friends,

I decided to write this book after viewing one of the most beautiful videos, the focus of which was being grateful for nature, love, and this life as a gift. In his video Brother David Steindl-Rast observes: (a Benedictine monk and author of Gratefulness, the Heart of Prayer)

"You think that this is just another day in your life... It's not just another day. It's the one day that is given to you - today. It's a gift. It's the only gift that you have right now, and the only appropriate response is gratefulness. If you learn to respond as if it were the first day in your life and the very last day then you will have spent this day very well.

Begin by opening your eyes, and be surprised that you have eyes you can open. That incredible array of colors that is constantly offered to us for our pure enjoyment. Look at the sky. We so rarely look at the sky. We so rarely note how different it is from moment to moment, with clouds coming and going.

Open your eyes. Look at that. Look at the faces of people whom you meet. Each one has an incredible story behind their face, Not only their own story, but the story of their ancestors. All that life from generations and from so many places all over the world flows together and meets you here like a life-giving water if you only open your heart and drink.

Open your heart to the incredible gifts that civilization gives to us. You flip a switch, and there is electric light. You turn a faucet, and there is warm water, and cold water, and drinkable water... a gift that millions and millions in the world will never experience.

And so I am wishing you will open your heart to all these blessings and let them flow through you. That everyone you will meet on this day will be blessed by you, just by your presence.

Let the gratefulness overflow into blessings all around you. Then it will really be a good day.

May your gratefulness overflow into blessings all around you, in deed.

After practising Gratitude for 28 days as suggested by Rhonda Byrne there was a sudden shift in my environment, people around me, my experiences and within me. The feelings brought a sense of depth and expansion to my life, allowing me to truly enjoy it. I've simply gathered all of that experience to share with you.

I don't consider myself an expert on the subject of gratitude. This book is simply an introduction—a gentle invitation to explore and adopt gratitude in your daily life. My hope is that, after reading it, you'll find more abundance, awareness, joy, and contentment in your journey. My gratitude to you for making this book a part of your beautiful journey.

Love,
Kinnari

Contents

The Story of Lord Krishna and Sudama

A timeless tale of gratitude, humility, and divine friendship!

Long ago in ancient India, there lived two boys—Krishna and Sudama—who studied together at the same Gurukul (school). Though they came from very different backgrounds, they were close friends. Krishna, the prince of Mathura, and Sudama, a poor Brahmin boy, shared food, stories, and dreams. Even after they grew up and went their separate ways, their bond remained strong.

Years later, Sudama was living in extreme poverty. He barely had enough to feed his children. His clothes were torn, and his house was falling apart. But he never complained. He stayed kind, humble, and full of devotion. His wife, seeing their condition, gently urged him to visit his old friend, Lord Krishna—now the mighty king of Dwarka—hoping he might offer help.

At first, Sudama was hesitant. He didn't want to beg or expect anything. But he agreed, not to ask for riches, but to see his friend again. Before leaving, his wife tied a small bundle of puffed rice—their only food—as a gift for Krishna, knowing it was his favorite.

When Sudama reached Krishna's palace, he was nervous and ashamed of his appearance. But Krishna, the ruler of a vast kingdom, ran barefoot to greet him. He embraced Sudama with deep love, washed his tired feet, and treated him like royalty. The palace was filled with joy.

Krishna asked, "What have you brought for me, dear friend?"

Sudama hesitated but slowly handed over the humble bundle of puffed rice. Krishna received it like it was a treasure. With every bite, his eyes sparkled—not because of the food's taste, but because of the love and gratitude it carried.

Sudama never asked for anything. Yet when he returned home, he found his hut transformed into a beautiful home, his children well-fed, and his life full of abundance.

This story shows that true gratitude doesn't come from wealth—it comes from the heart. Sudama never expected anything, yet he offered the best he had with love. And Krishna, touched by his friend's simple offering, gave him more than he ever asked for.

Gratitude, when expressed sincerely, has the power to transform lives. It nurtures relationships, melts pride, and connects hearts beyond status or riches.

"It's not happiness that brings us gratitude, it's gratitude that brings us happiness."

Another True Story : Oprah Winfrey— Gratitude Despite the Odds

Oprah Winfrey's journey is one of the most inspiring stories in the world, not just because of her incredible success, but because of how she built her life on a foundation of self-belief, forgiveness, and **deep gratitude** for everything she experienced, even the painful parts.

Born in Mississippi in 1954 into extreme poverty, Oprah had a difficult childhood. She faced abuse, instability, and many emotional challenges growing up. For years, she lived with her grandmother, who was so poor that Oprah wore dresses made from potato sacks. At one point in her childhood, she moved between different homes and even experienced rejection from her own mother.

But instead of letting these hardships define her in bitterness, Oprah later said that she chose to be **grateful for the lessons they taught her**. She believed that every struggle helped shape her strength, empathy, and compassion. One of Oprah's most famous quotes is:

"Be thankful for what you have; you will end up having more. If you concentrate on what you don't have, you will never, ever have enough."

Throughout her life, she maintained a gratitude journal, where she wrote five things every day that she was thankful for—even during difficult times. She credited this small, simple practice with completely changing her mindset and creating more peace and abundance in her life.

Today, Oprah is one of the most influential women in the world—a billionaire, media mogul, philanthropist, and spiritual voice to millions. Yet she often says that gratitude is still the single most powerful tool she uses daily. It helped her rise above her past, connect deeply with others, and remain grounded despite her success.

Why this story matters:

Oprah's life shows us that *gratitude isn't only about feeling thankful when things go well*—it's about finding meaning and growth even in the pain. She didn't wait for her life to become perfect before being grateful. Instead, she made gratitude a habit—and that habit shaped her destiny.

Whether you're in a small village or a big city, rich or poor, struggling or succeeding—Oprah's story reminds us that *gratitude is the doorway to hope, healing, and true abundance*.

Introduction: The Power of Gratitude in Rewiring Your Mind and Rising Above Challenges

"Gratitude is not only the greatest of virtues, but the parent of all the others."

\- Marcus Tullius Cicero

What is Gratitude?

I will be sharing my learning's on this subject with you.

Gratitude is a profound human emotion, a mindset, and a practice that has the power to transform our lives. An emotion similar to appreciation. It is like being in state of happiness and thankfulness in response to something. It's more than just saying "thank you".

At it's core, gratitude is the recognition and appreciation of life's blessings, whether tangible or intangible. It is more than just saying "thank you" or expressing politeness; it is an intentional focus on the positives, fostering a sense of acknowledgment for what we often take for granted. Gratitude is a celebration of life's blessings, both big and small, shifting our perspective from lack to abundance, from despair to hope, and dissatisfaction to contentment. It is a profound acknowledgment of kindness, a universal balm that heals and connects.

According to Robert A. Emmons, one of the key proponents in the field of gratitude research, gratitude has two core components—first as “an affirmation of goodness" and then as a way for us to acknowledge that the “sources of this goodness lie outside ourselves" (Emmons, 2010). These two stages of gratitude comprise the recognition of goodness and then an understanding of how did this goodness come to us. This description of gratitude is quite similar to the one provided by Brother David Steindl-Rast, a Benedictine monk and author of Gratefulness, the Heart of Prayer. According to Brother David, gratefulness has two important qualities, the first being the appreciation of something you deem valuable.The second quality of gratefulness is that it must be gratis or given freely (The Gratefulness Team, 2017).

Gratitude can beautifully be compared to a flourishing garden, where each expression of thankfulness represents a unique plant or flower. In no time you will realize that you have a beautiful garden with all kind of pretty, colourful and lovely flowers growing in it which not only has the best of fragrances but also a sight that you would not want to take your eyes off.

With every seed planted, weed removed, and flower you nurtured, you’re not just tending a garden—you’re cultivating a life rooted in gratitude.

The Science of Gratitude and It’s Impact on the Brain

Evidence-Backed: The Feedback Loop of Gratitude

Gratitude creates a feedback loop that reinforces itself. Here’s how:

As Misty Pratt writes in her Mindful.org article “The Science of Gratitude” (February, 2022):

"Research shows gratitude isn't just a pleasant feeling— it also supports greater health, happiness, and wisdom in ourselves and our communities."

Over the past two decades, a growing body of evidence in the field of social science has revealed gratitude's measurable benefits across nearly every aspect of life. Gratitude appears to contribute substantially to individual well-being and physical health so significantly that the Greater Good Science Center at the University of California, Berkeley—a leader in research on the science of social and emotional well-being—describes gratitude as the "social glue" essential for building and nurturing strong relationships.

The Science: Stronger Connections

"Social connection is likely a key to well-being," says Lisa Walsh*. She explains that gratitude might not be an emotion that just makes people feel good; it appears to have social implications by motivating individuals to improve themselves.

In an upcoming study from the PAW Laboratory at UC-Riverside, high school students who expressed gratitude had a mixed experience—they felt "elevated" (a positive emotion) and indebted. Immediately after writing their gratitude letters, the students also felt motivated to improve themselves.

More on Gratitude Scientifically

1. Neurological Basis: Gratitude activates the brain's reward system, including the ventromedial prefrontal cortex, which is linked to decision-making and social cognition. When

* Lisa C. Walsh is a social and personality psychologist specializing in happiness, gratitude, and well-being research. She earned her Ph.D. in Social/Personality Psychology from the University of California, Riverside, under the mentorship of Dr. Sonja Lyubomirsky in the Positive Activities and Well-Being (PAW) Laboratory. For more information please visit www.lisacwalsh.com

you practice gratitude, your brain releases dopamine and serotonin—chemicals that enhance mood and make you want to repeat the behavior.

2. Rewiring the Brain: Regular gratitude practice strengthens neural pathways associated with positive thinking, making it easier to notice and appreciate good things in life.
3. Social Reinforcement: Expressing gratitude deepens relationships, creating a cycle of mutual appreciation. People who feel appreciated are more likely to reciprocate, sustaining a continuous exchange of gratitude.

Study Highlight:

A 2016 NeuroImage* study demonstrated lasting changes in brain activity for participants who wrote gratitude letters even weeks later. This suggests that gratitude has long-term effects on mental health and happiness.

Gratitude is nature's magnetic force, when nurtured, draws in more reasons to be grateful. It's not just a feel-good emotion, but a practice that creates a cycle of positivity and abundance. Like ripples spreading across a pond, gratitude radiates outward, influencing our mindset, relationships, and even the world around us. This chapter explores the magic of this cycle, backed by science, metaphors, real-life examples, and practical insights.

The Ripple Effect of Gratitude

Imagine that you are throwing a pebble into still water, the ripples spread outward, touching everything in their surroundings and everything in their path. Gratitude works the same way. The moment you feel or express gratitude, it creates ripples that will not only change your perspective, uplifting you and those around you, but also attract similar positive energy back into your life.

---

* A 2016 study published in NeuroImage by Prathik Kini and colleagues at Indiana University explored the neural effects of gratitude expression.

Example: The Gratitude Chain

Consider a workplace where a manager consistently thanks their team for their efforts. This acknowledgment makes the team feel valued, and they feel motivated to perform better, thus inspiring them to work more effectively. In return, they express gratitude towards those around them, their colleagues and friends. The positivity snowballs, creating a supportive and productive environment where everyone feels valued and appreciated.

The Law of Attraction and Gratitude

In the realm of metaphysics, gratitude is often linked to the Law of Attraction, which suggests that like attracts like. By focusing on what you're grateful for, you align your energy with abundance, inviting more blessings into your life.

Gratitude as a Beacon

Think of gratitude as a lighthouse in the fog of life. When you shine your light of appreciation, it not only illuminates the blessings you already have but also acts as a signal, attracting new opportunities, relationships, and experiences.

Gratitude Must Be Intentional

Gratitude is an intentional practice rather than an automatic reaction. Most people believe that they automatically thank a situation, person or even their God, but true gratitude requires intentional action and a conscious effort to remain grateful most of the time, if not always. They believe that their reaction is always Gratitude and it happens naturally when something good happens. For Example, if someone gives you a gift or helps you, you say "**thank you**" and move on. However, this is **passive** and dependent on **external circumstances**.

Gratitude must be **intentional**. It is not just a response to good things, but a deliberate choice to see the good, even in ordinary or difficult moments. It is about actively looking for reasons to appreciate life, even on your bad days.

On days when we feel that nothing good is happening, we must appreciate all the things we already have.

We should acknowledge what we have received so far, which could be as simple as appreciating the food, shelter and clothing that we have had besides anything else that is luxurious in our life and appreciating that and expressing gratitude for those things too.

Example:

- Imagine two people stuck in traffic.
  - One person complains about the delay.
  - The other takes a deep breath and thinks, "I am grateful for this extra time to listen to my favorite podcast or call my friend to catch up".

The "Rewire" Concept of this book title: Using Gratitude to Rewire Your Thought Patterns

Our brains are wired to focus on problems—a survival instinct known as the *negativity bias*. This makes us dwell on what's missing rather than appreciating what we have. However, gratitude rewires the brain by strengthening neural pathways that recognize abundance. Like a muscle, the more we practice gratitude—by noticing small joys, reframing challenges, and appreciating daily blessings—the easier it becomes to see the good in life. Over time, gratitude shifts our mindset from scarcity to abundance, making us naturally more positive, resilient, and fulfilled. It's not about ignoring difficulties but training the brain to find what's already enough.

Example:

- If you receive nine compliments and one criticism, what do you dwell on?
  - Most people fixate on the one negative comment, ignoring the nine positives.
  - That is the brain's negativity bias at work.

How Gratitude Rewires the Brain to Notice Abundance

- The more we **intentionally focus on what's good,** the more the brain strengthens those neural pathways.
- This is called **neuroplasticity**—the brain's ability to rewire itself based on what we repeatedly focus on.

The good news is that we can train our brain by practicing gratitude. Gratitude trains the brain to focus on what's present rather than what's missing. Through this process, the brain strengthens pathways linked to appreciation and positivity, making gratitude a default mindset over time.

Let me make it simple for you to understand. To start with, *neuroplasticity* is your brain's *ability to change, grow, and adapt* based on what you do, think, and experience.

Think of your brain like a network of roads. Every time you think a certain way or do something repeatedly, you're building and strengthening those roads. The more often you use a road (or thought pattern), the smoother and faster it gets. If you stop using a road, it fades over time. So basically: *Your brain can rewire itself—at any age.*

Here's how. For beginners, let's understand how gratitude helps neuroplasticity

When you practice gratitude regularly (like noticing and appreciating the good in your day), your brain starts building stronger "*positive*" pathways.

More often we humans tend to always focus on stress, criticism, self- limitations or negativity. For example, you may catch yourself thinking, “I don’t have good job”, “I don’t have enough money” or “Nothing is going good in my life”. These thoughts don’t help in making the situation any better or you feel any better, it just works against you. If you acknowledge all the things you have in your life and start being thankful for them, your brain’s attention will learn to focus on the good stuff.

As Tony Robbins* says, “*Energy flows where attention goes.*” Once you focus your energy on the positives in your life, amazing things start to happen. Choosing gratitude and appreciation over criticism and negativity leads to attracting more of the things you can appreciate and be grateful for. When you look at your mornings do you see lovely sun shining or do you see a sun which has lost it’s shine? If you focus on the positives, you’ll radiate confidence and attract all things positive around you. You’ll feel more optimistic and hopeful and this happens because you're *rewiring your brain to notice and expect positive experiences*, which is *neuroplasticity in action.*

Neuroplasticity is the brain’s ability to reorganize and form new connections based on our thoughts and habits. When we focus on problems, the brain strengthens negative pathways, making stress and scarcity our default. But practicing gratitude rewires the brain by strengthening positive neural circuits, helping us naturally notice abundance.

Gratitude activates the prefrontal cortex, which improves emotional control and decision-making. It also boosts dopamine and serotonin, the brain’s “happiness chemicals.” Like a well-used path, the more we practice gratitude, the stronger it becomes—helping us feel happier, more resilient, and more optimistic over

* Tony Robbins is a well-known American author, entrepreneur, philanthropist, and life coach. He is widely recognized for his motivational speaking and self-help books that focus on personal development, success, and peak performance. Author of books named Awaken the Giant Within, Unlimited Power etc

time. Studies show that practicing gratitude increases activity in the prefrontal cortex, the area responsible for emotional regulation and decision-making. Over time, people who practice gratitude experience more positive emotions naturally—without forcing it.

Example:

- Think of the brain like a hiking trail. If you keep walking the negativity path, it becomes well-worn and automatic.
- But if you start walking the gratitude path daily, over time, the old path grows over, and the new one becomes your default as it becomes clearer and stronger.
- The brain literally rewires itself to notice abundance, build resilience, and create lasting emotional well-being rather than scarcity.

The "Rise" Concept of this book title: Using Gratitude to Elevate Your Life

Gratitude isn't just about feeling thankful—it's a *powerful tool for growth and transformation*. When practiced intentionally, gratitude shifts your mindset from limitation to possibility, helping you rise above challenges with resilience and optimism. It fosters a deeper appreciation for life, strengthens relationships, and enhances emotional well-being. Gratitude also fuels motivation by helping you see progress rather than setbacks. By focusing on what's already good, you create a strong foundation for *personal growth, confidence, and success*. The more you practice gratitude, the higher you rise—unlocking a life filled with purpose, joy, and fulfillment.

Using Gratitude to Elevate Your Life

You must have come across several powerful tools and habits people commonly use to elevate their lives—meaning to improve their mindset, well-being, relationships, and overall success.

Some of the most common ones are positive thinking, self-discipline, mindfulness and meditation, exercise, healthy living, lifelong learning, kindness and service, setting goals and taking actions.

Using Gratitude to Elevate Your Life means harnessing the power of thankfulness to improve the way you think, feel, and live. When you focus on what you do have, instead of what you don't have, your mindset starts to change. You feel more positive, calm, and motivated. Gratitude helps you notice the good in your life—even small things like a kind message, a hot meal, or your connection with outside world through Wi-Fi.

This shift can lift you up when life feels heavy. It helps you deal with stress, grow through challenges, and see opportunities more clearly. Instead of getting stuck in negativity, gratitude reminds you that there's still something to smile about.

Elevating your life doesn't mean being rich or perfect—it means feeling more fulfilled, connected, and happy. Gratitude is a free tool that anyone can use. And the more you use it, the more it changes your outlook, your relationships, and your future.

So, "using gratitude to elevate your life" simply means choosing to appreciate the good, and letting that mindset lift you higher in every part of your journey.

CONCLUSION

- Newton's law states: "For every action, there is an equal and opposite reaction." When you apply the idea of Gratitude to Newton's law it means, "Every action of giving thanks always causes the opposite action of receiving."

"Feeling gratitude and not expressing it is like wrapping a present and not giving it."

- William Arthur Ward

Part 1:

Rewiring Your Mind with Gratitude

Chapter 1

The Gratitude Brain – How It Shapes Your Thoughts

"Gratitude is the most exquisite form of courtesy."

- Jacques Maritain

What if the key to transforming your life isn't changing your circumstances—but changing your brain's focus?

Dr. Rick Hanson, Neuropsychologist, Author of Hardwiring Happiness explains: "The brain takes it's shape from what the mind rests upon." This means that focusing on positive experiences (like gratitude) helps rewire the brain toward happiness and resilience. It's clear that you can reshape your brain by intentionally focusing on positive experiences, supporting the idea that changing your brain's focus leads to lasting transformation.

Here are some more reference from famous author's books on this topic:

Dr. Joe Dispenza in 'Breaking the Habit of Being Yourself' explains how thinking differently rewires the brain and changes our reality emphasizing that internal focus creates external change.

Your brain is like a garden—whatever you plant and nurture will grow. If you constantly focus on problems, stress, and negativity, those neural pathways become stronger, making it easier to dwell on what's wrong. But when you intentionally practice gratitude, you rewire your brain to recognize and appreciate the good, fostering a more positive, resilient, and abundant mindset.

The Commute That Changed Everything

Let's understand this concept a little further through Maya's Story:

Every morning, Maya faced the same thing—traffic, noise, and stress during her long commute to work. She would grip the steering wheel tightly, her mind already dreading the day ahead. By the time she arrived at the office, her mood was drained. This was her routine—an automatic cycle of frustration that seemed impossible to break. One day, after reading about gratitude and neuroplasticity, Maya decided to experiment. Instead of listening to the usual news or venting to herself about traffic, she began using that time to mentally list five things she was grateful for. At first, it felt forced. She repeated basic things like "I'm thankful for my job" or "I'm grateful for coffee." The best thing she did was that she kept at it.

Over a few days, something subtle but powerful began to shift.

She started noticing the beauty of morning light through her windshield. She felt more appreciative of the silence before emails and meetings. Even when traffic was bad, her reactions softened. The irritation didn't consume her like before. Her mind was rewiring—creating new patterns that prioritized calm, presence, and gratitude over stress and autopilot frustration. By consistently choosing to focus on what was going right instead of what was wrong, Maya didn't just change her mornings and the days—she changed her mind. She literally trained her brain to default to peace instead of panic—demonstrating neuroplasticity in action.

Gratitude in Action: Training Your Brain for Positivity

This transformation happens because of neuroplasticity, the brain's ability to reshape itself based on repeated thoughts and behaviors. When you focus on gratitude daily—whether through journaling, affirmations, or mindful moments of appreciation—your brain strengthens the pathways associated with positivity, contentment, and emotional well-being. Over time, gratitude becomes second nature, making optimism your default mode of thinking.

The human brain is naturally more sensitive to negative information—this is known as the *negativity bias.* It helped our ancestors survive by paying closer attention to danger, but today, it often keeps us stuck in stress, anxiety, and fear. Gratitude works as a counterbalance. By intentionally focusing on what's good, even in tough moments, we train our brain to shift away from fear-based thinking and toward appreciation, opportunity, and resilience.

Instead of dwelling on what's missing or going wrong, a gratitude-trained brain naturally sees opportunities, small joys, and silver linings—even in challenges.

Studies from leading universities like UC Berkeley and Harvard show that gratitude practices:

- Increases activity in the prefrontal cortex (responsible for decision-making, emotional regulation, and planning).
- Reduces activity in the amygdala (linked to fear and stress).

This rewiring isn't just emotional—it's physical.

This mindset shift also strengthens mental resilience. Grateful people usually cope better with stress, recover faster from setbacks, and maintain a more balanced perspective during hardships. Studies show that gratitude activates the prefrontal cortex, the part of the brain responsible for decision-making and emotional regulation. By rewiring your brain with gratitude, you develop an inner strength that allows you to rise above difficulties with grace and optimism.

Gratitude isn't just about feeling good in the moment—it's a mental habit that shapes your thoughts, emotions, and overall outlook on life, helping you rewire and rise with confidence and clarity.

"The most beautiful moments in life are moments when you are expressing joy, not when you are seeking it."

— Jaggi Vasudev

The Link Between Gratitude and Mental Resilience

Why do some people remain calm and hopeful when life falls apart—while others crumble under pressure?

The answer lies in mental resilience—the inner strength that helps you recover, adapt, and grow. Surprisingly, one of the most powerful tools to build this resilience isn't toughness or denial—it's gratitude. It's how quickly your mind returns to hope. That's where gratitude becomes your inner shield.

In challenging times, some people seem to bounce back more easily, adapt with grace, and find light in dark moments. This ability isn't luck—it's called mental resilience, and one of the most overlooked yet powerful tools to build it, is gratitude.

One's mental resilience is strengthened through gratitude as it helps the brain develop healthier and more balanced thought processes. Our negative emotions are amplified and narrow our focus when faced with any sort of stress, uncertainty, or loss. That is when the brain immediately defaults to fear-based responses. Now, here's the kicker! Gratitude works in a different direction.

Even when much feels off and broken, gratitude lends a helping hand in broadening your perspective, often encouraging calm thinking and helping you identify what's still working for you.

Neuroscience can back this mental shift. Practicing gratitude activates the prefrontal cortex. This area of the brain governs emotional regulation and proceeds to indicate a calming activity in the amygdala, which is the centre of fear and emotional reactivity in our brains. Consistently practicing gratitude rewires our brain; it forms new neural pathways in our brains, allowing us to become more adaptable and less responsive to stress.

Resilience doesn't mean you're unaffected by difficulties. It means you're equipped to move through them, without being consumed. Gratitude doesn't erase the pain of loss, failure, or disappointment but it gives you an anchor—a way to stay mentally steady when everything around you feels unstable.

Consider a person who loses their job unexpectedly. A reactive mind might spiral into panic: "I'm a failure. I'll never recover." But a gratitude-trained mind may, after the initial shock, begin to recognize small positives: "At least I have savings. I'm not alone. Maybe this is the change I needed." That simple redirection changes not just mood—but also the ability to think clearly, make good decisions, and stay emotionally grounded.

Even in everyday stress, gratitude builds resilience. People who regularly practice gratitude report better sleep, stronger relationships, lower levels of depression, and increased optimism—all of which are key ingredients for handling life's curveballs.

And here's the best part: building resilience through gratitude doesn't require big, dramatic efforts. It can be as simple as writing down three things you're thankful for before bed, taking a deep breath and noticing what's okay in the present moment, or expressing appreciation to someone. These small acts, repeated over time, shape a stronger, more centered mind.

In essence, gratitude trains your brain to become more flexible, less reactive, and more hopeful. It doesn't just make you feel good in peaceful times—it prepares you to stand tall in the storm. That's the true power of mental resilience—and gratitude is the root.

Let me share a story that I once read about a sportsperson

Tennis player Novak Djokovic has spoken about the role gratitude plays in his mental game. After tough matches, injuries, or defeats, he takes time to reflect on what he's thankful for—his health, support team, or the opportunity to compete at all.

Djokovic attributes much of his emotional control and comeback ability to mindfulness and gratitude practices. After a major injury in 2017, instead of falling into frustration, he focused on gratitude for his body's ability to heal and the lessons learned from the break. This mindset helped him make a powerful return to the top of his game.

"Gratitude changes your perspective. When I feel grateful, I feel more calm, more present, and more focused."

— Novak Djokovic

Summary

- Gratitude rewires your brain — it strengthens pathways for calm, clarity, and emotional resilience.
- Focusing on what's going right helps shift your mindset from scarcity and stress to abundance and peace.
- Even small daily habits—like writing down three things you're grateful for—can create lasting transformation.
- Maya's story shows how simple changes (like a gratitude practice during a stressful commute) can reshape your emotional experience.

- Scientific research confirms that gratitude activates the prefrontal cortex (for emotional balance) and reduces stress signals from the amygdala.
- Gratitude doesn't ignore difficulties—it helps you rise above them with grace and maintain perspective.
- It's not about perfect moments—it's about training your mind to see the good even in imperfect ones.
- Ask yourself each day, "What am I thankful for today?" That question is powerful enough to start real change.
- Gratitude is not a moment—it is a mindset. And it's how you rise.

Chapter 2

Breaking Mental Barriers with Gratitude

"Gratitude is the healthiest of all human emotions. The more you express gratitude for what you have, the more likely you will have even more to express gratitude for."

- Zig Ziglar

What if the only thing holding you back isn't the world—but the story you keep telling yourself?

The Invisible Wall

Let me share a story about a young girl Meera who was working with me in my office, where we attended to the various customer queries about loans for car purchases. My colleague Meera was a talented artist who had a dream of showcasing her work in a gallery since college. She painted every day, filling sketchbooks and canvases with powerful pieces. But every time someone suggested she apply to an exhibit or share her work online, she hesitated.

"I'm not good enough."

"What if people criticize me?"

"Real artists have degrees from fancy schools."

These thoughts echoed in her mind as if they were true, even though they were just old beliefs she had absorbed from a childhood where creativity was dismissed as a hobby, not a career. Deep down, Meera feared failure, so she stayed safe—sharing her art only with close friends, declining opportunities, and telling herself she was just "not ready yet."

Years passed, and she watched others who were less experienced gain recognition. She wasn't moving ahead, not because of lack of talent, but because she was unknowingly trapping herself behind the invisible wall of her self-limiting beliefs.

Only when a mentor gently challenged her thoughts—asking, "What if your fear isn't the truth, just a habit?"—did Meera begin to question the stories she was telling herself. That shift in mindset became the first crack in the wall.

After her mentor's question, Meera felt something stir—a quiet discomfort with the excuses she'd been telling herself. She went home and, instead of picking up her paintbrush, she picked up a notebook and wrote:

"Today, I'm grateful for the courage to question my own doubts."

The next day, she wrote:

"I'm grateful for the hands that allow me to create."

And on the third day:

"I'm thankful for the few people who already believe in me, even when I don't."

This daily gratitude practice began to transform her deeply. Slowly, her focus moved from fear to strength—from "What if I fail?" to "What if I inspire someone?"

Within weeks, Meera shared a piece of art online with the caption: "This one helped me heal." The response was encouraging, so she shared more.

Each act of gratitude chipped away at the invisible wall of self-doubt. It didn't disappear overnight—but it cracked enough for her to move through.

Eventually, Meera submitted her portfolio to a local gallery. When they accepted her work, she cried—not just from joy, but from relief. She hadn't waited to feel fearless. She had simply chosen to be grateful, and that opened the door.

I've read books and heard in recordings from speakers like Zig Ziglar, who said, ***"You don't have to be great to start, but you have to start to be great."*** Take small, consistent steps toward your goals, and don't be afraid to step out of your comfort zone. Every action you take brings you closer to success. Even famous speaker Tony Robbins frequently emphasizes how positive thinking profoundly affects outcomes. He says it's key to focus on the good stuff, even when things get tough.

Breaking Mental Barriers with Gratitude

Stories like Meera's aren't rare—they're happening quietly in the minds of many people who are capable, creative, and full of potential, yet stuck behind invisible walls made of self-doubt, fear, or old beliefs. These walls don't break with force—they break with awareness. Gratitude is one of the simplest, most powerful tools to begin.

When you practice gratitude regularly, you shift your inner dialogue. Instead of replaying what's missing, wrong, or broken, your mind begins to recognize what's working, present, and possible. This shift isn't just emotional—it's neurological. Gratitude activates the brain regions responsible for clarity, optimism, and decision-making, weakening the power of old, fear-based thought loops.

Gratitude also helps you distance yourself from harsh self-judgment. You begin to see yourself not just as someone who isn't there yet, but someone who is growing, showing up, and doing the best they can. This more compassionate perspective helps you move from paralysis to progress.

You don't need a perfect plan or total confidence to begin. You just need a mindful moment—and one thing to be thankful for. That small shift, repeated daily, clears mental fog and plants courage.

How Gratitude Works

Gratitude might seem like just saying "thank you," but it's far more powerful—it's a mental habit that reshapes your thinking. When you focus on what's going well (even in small ways), your brain starts building new thought patterns that recognize opportunities, not just problems.

Limiting beliefs like "I'm not good enough" or "I'll never succeed"—often come from fear or past experiences. Gratitude doesn't ignore those feelings, but it gently shifts your focus. It helps you see what's working, what you already have, and how you've grown. This perspective weakens fear and builds confidence.

"You don't need to feel ready—you just need to feel grateful."

- Unknown

Example: If you constantly think, "I don't have what it takes to succeed," try writing down one good thing you have done, each day - even small things like helping a friend, finishing a task, or learning something—new. Over time, your brain begins to see yourself differently—not as someone who's failing, but as someone who's progressing.

Gratitude doesn't erase struggle but gives you the mental strength to move through it with more hope and courage and above all belief in yourself that you can definitely do it.

The Recipe for Change: Gratitude Over Fear

Ravi dreamt of starting his own café but believed success was only for the rich or well-connected. "People like me don't build businesses," he told himself, stuck in a safe, unfulfilling job. One day, a friend praised his hosting skills and said that people love his food. That night, Ravi wrote, "I'm grateful for the gift of making people feel at home." That small shift changed everything. He started a weekend food stall. Months later, it became a café. His belief didn't change first—his focus did. Gratitude helped him see possibility where fear once lived.

Ravi's journey reminds us that change doesn't begin with perfect conditions—it begins with a shift in mindset. Gratitude didn't give him a business plan, but it gave him belief. When we choose to see our gifts instead of our gaps, we unlock courage to take the first real step forward.

You don't need to feel fearless to begin—just be grateful enough to see what's possible.

Start by acknowledging your strengths, no matter how ordinary they seem. Gratitude shifts your focus from limitations to potential.

Ask yourself: What am I good at that I haven't given myself enough credit for? That's your starting point

"They can because they think they can"

- Virgil

Our minds are often shaped by deep-seated beliefs and thought patterns that influence how we see ourselves and the world. Many of these beliefs act as mental barriers, limiting our growth, confidence, and ability to embrace life's opportunities. These self-imposed limitations often stem from past experiences, societal conditioning, or fear of failure.

Gratitude serves as a powerful tool to break these barriers by shifting focus from what we lack to what we have. It challenges negative thought patterns, rewires the brain for positivity, and opens the door to growth, self-acceptance, and new possibilities. When we actively practice gratitude, we create a mindset shift that helps us see setbacks as lessons, failures as stepping stones, and challenges as opportunities to rise.

Self - Limiting beliefs and Identifying them

Now let's first understand what self-limiting beliefs are. These are negative thoughts or assumptions we hold about ourselves that restrict our potential. These are the quiet inner voices that say, "I'm not good enough," "I'll fail anyway," or "This isn't meant for people like me." They often run in the background of our minds and influence our choices, behaviors, and self-worth—without us even realizing it.

But where do they come from?

Most self-limiting beliefs are shaped by past experiences, upbringing, cultural messages, and repeated thoughts. They can stem from early failures, criticism, comparisons, or emotional wounds. Over time, these beliefs settle in like default settings in the mind.

How can you tell you're operating from a self-limiting belief?

Look for patterns like procrastination, fear of failure, staying in your comfort zone, or doubting yourself often—even when you have the skills or opportunities.

To identify them, start by observing your self-talk. Ask yourself:

- "What do I believe about myself in this situation?"
- "Is this belief helping me grow or holding me back?"

- "Would I say this to someone I care about?"

Awareness is the first step. Once you spot these beliefs, gratitude can help challenge and replace them with empowering truths.

One of the most effective ways to break mental barriers is through *gratitude journaling.* This practice allows us to identify and reframe limiting beliefs by recognizing the abundance, strengths, and opportunities already present in our lives. By consistently recording moments of gratitude, we create a new mental framework that fosters self-belief, resilience, and an empowered mindset—allowing us to rewire our thoughts and rise beyond our limitations.

Let's look at practical examples

1. Belief: "I'm not smart enough to succeed in my career."
    - Where It Comes From: Past failures, comparisons to others, or critical feedback.
    - Reframing with Gratitude: "I'm grateful for my willingness to learn and grow. Every challenge is an opportunity to improve."
2. Belief: "I don't deserve happiness or success."
    - Where It Comes From: Low self-esteem, past mistakes, or negative conditioning.
    - Reframing with Gratitude: "I'm grateful for the progress I've made and the opportunities ahead."

Using Gratitude to Challenge and Replace Negative Thought Patterns

Negative thoughts can become automatic, reinforcing feelings of self-doubt, fear, and scarcity. Let's see how we can change this kind of thought process.

For example, instead of thinking this:

Negative Thought: "I'll never succeed,"

- Gratitude shifts the focus to "I'm grateful for the progress I've made and the lessons I've learned."

Negative Thought: "People don't appreciate me."

- Gratitude Shift: "I am grateful for the people who do support and value me. I also appreciate myself and what I bring to others."

Negative Thought: "I always fail at new things."

- Gratitude Shift: "Every failure has taught me something valuable. I'm grateful for the chance to learn and improve."

Negative Thought: "Nobody supports me."

- Gratitude Shift: "I am grateful for the people who do care about me, even if it's just one or two. I also appreciate my own strength and ability to support myself."

Negative Thought: "I don't have enough time to take care of myself."

- Gratitude Shift: "I'm grateful for the moments I do have, and I will use them wisely to nurture myself, even in small ways."

Negative Thought: "I'm too old to start something new."

- Gratitude Shift: "I'm grateful for my experiences, which give me wisdom and confidence. Every day is a chance to grow and try something new."

Negative Thought: "I'll never be as successful as others."

- Gratitude Shift: "I'm grateful for my own unique journey. Success is personal, and I appreciate the progress I've made in my own way."

Negative Thought: “My life is so ordinary; there’s nothing special about it.”

- Gratitude Shift: “I’m grateful for the simple joys in my life sunrises, laughter and small moments of happiness that make life meaningful.”

Negative Thought: “I’m not as good as others at [skill or job].”

- Gratitude. Shift: “I’m grateful for the opportunity to learn and grow. Improvement is a journey, and I appreciate the progress I’ve made.

Small changes in the way you think can make a big difference over time. When you stop putting yourself down and start being thankful for what you have and who you are, your brain starts to feel more positive and strong. Your efforts of gradually replacing negative statements or talks with yourself that hold you back to more positive ones which support your growth and confidence will create a ripple effect. This weakens negative pathways in your brain and it gets easier to break those pathways and form new positive pathways which ignite optimism and courage.

Gratitude helps you stop focusing on fear and start believing in yourself.

The Gratitude Journaling Technique for Mindset Shifts

Gratitude journaling is a simple yet powerful practice to rewire the brain for positivity. By consistently writing down what you’re grateful for, you train your mind to focus on abundance rather than scarcity. This practice shifts perspectives, helping to overcome self-doubt, increase self-awareness, and reinforce positive thought patterns.

A practical method is the 3-2-1 technique:

- 3 things you're grateful for today
- 2 ways you've grown recently
- 1 positive self-affirmation

Over time, this habit reshapes your mindset, breaks mental barriers, and cultivates lasting self-belief and inner strength, allowing you to rise beyond your limitations.

Try This: 3-2-1 Gratitude Journal (Daily Practice)

Prompt	Example Entry
3 things you're grateful for	"Morning walk, mom's smile, a friend's message"
2 ways you've grown	"I speak up more. I'm learning to be patient."
1 kind thought to yourself	"I am powerful. I am worthy."

This technique trains your mind to notice what's working instead of what's lacking—building self-worth and positive focus.

From Fear to Possibility: Mindset Shift Path

Old Thought	Gratitude Shift
"I'm not good enough."	"I'm grateful for my effort and my growth."
"I always fail."	"I'm thankful for what failure has taught me."
"People don't support me."	"I'm grateful for those who do—and for my inner strength."
"I'm too old/young to begin."	"I'm thankful it's never too late to grow."

Summary of Breaking Mental Barriers with Gratitude

- Self-limiting beliefs are like invisible walls built from fear, doubt, or old experiences.
- Gratitude is a tool that gently cracks these walls by shifting your focus to what's good, possible, and already within you.
- Repeating small acts of gratitude helps rewire your brain to think more positively and build confidence.
- You don't need to be fearless to start—you just need to focus on your strengths and the present moment.

Chapter 3

The Science of Emotional Regulation

"Gratitude becomes your inner compass, guiding you through storms—not by avoiding them, but by helping you rise above them."

- Kinnari Sonchhatra

Have you ever wondered why a single comment can ruin your entire day, or how a small win can lift your spirits for hours?

That's the power of emotions—they shape how we experience life and influence our behavior, which impacts every aspect of our well-being. Emotions guide the decisions we make, affecting our relationships, career progress, and even our health. They serve as internal signals, helping us understand what we're feeling, why we're feeling it, and what we might need to do next. Think of them like the dashboard lights in a car—when something flashes, it's a sign to pay attention.

Emotions are like messengers—they give us clues about how we feel and how we're responding to our environment, people, situations, work, relationships, and the world around us. For example, fear might warn you of danger, joy can highlight what matters to you, and sadness encourages you to slow down and reflect. Emotions influence our decisions, relationships, motivation, and overall mental health. Ignoring or suppressing emotions can lead to stress and confusion, while learning to understand and express them in healthy ways builds emotional strength and resilience. Emotions also shape how we perceive the world and influence how we approach tasks and challenges.

The Magic of Emotions and Self - regulation

The Day Riya Almost Quit – and Chose Gratitude Instead

Riya was a bright, thoughtful student who loved taking part in group projects. One day, during a school presentation meeting, she shared an idea she was really proud of. But her teammates quickly dismissed it and moved on. Riya felt a wave of anger, hurt, and rejection. For the rest of the day, she kept thinking, "They don't value me. Maybe I'm not good enough."

That evening, still upset, Riya opened her gratitude journal—a habit she had started a few weeks earlier. She wasn't in the mood, but she tried anyway.

She wrote:

- *"I'm grateful for the chance to speak up, even if it didn't go as I hoped."*
- *"I'm grateful that I care enough about this project to feel this strongly."*
- *"I'm grateful for the ability to reflect before reacting."*

As she wrote, her mind began to shift. Her emotions, once heavy, began to feel more like clues than enemies. She realized her sadness showed how much she cared about being heard, and her anger revealed a need for mutual respect.

The next day, Riya calmly shared with her group how she felt. To her surprise, her teammates apologized—they hadn't meant to ignore her. They invited her to explain her idea again, and this time, they listened. Not only did her idea become part of the final project, but the group worked better together afterward.

By using gratitude, Riya didn't let her emotions control her—but she didn't ignore them either. Gratitude gave her the *clarity* to see the lesson in the moment, the courage to speak up, and the resilience to stay engaged instead of walking away.

In short, emotions are not problems—they're powerful guides. When we learn to work with them instead of against them, we cultivate a healthier mind and a more balanced life. By listening to our emotions, we gain valuable insights into our thoughts, behaviors, and choices. Emotional awareness is the first step toward mental well-being. When we understand, manage, and respond to our emotions in healthy ways, we build inner balance, resilience, and peace.

Human emotions are complex and varied, encompassing everything from joy and happiness to sadness, anger, fear, and many more. Managing these emotions begins with understanding their triggers, accepting them without judgment, and developing healthy coping mechanisms. Practices like mindfulness, deep breathing, journaling, and seeking professional help can be beneficial and promote emotional well-being.

Letters of Light

I'd like to share with you the story of Ananya who had always been close to her childhood friend, Meera. But over the years, their bond weakened due to misunderstandings and unspoken hurt. Ananya often felt a rush of irritation whenever she thought about Meera. She replayed old arguments in her head and avoided any chance of reconnecting.

One evening, while journaling in her new gratitude diary, Ananya wrote: "I'm thankful for old friendships that shaped me."

The simple line brought tears to her eyes. She started recalling the good times: the support Meera gave during her exams, the long phone calls, the birthdays remembered.

Over the next few days, Ananya continued writing one thing she was grateful for in that relationship. It didn't erase the hurt, but it softened her perspective. With greater emotional calm, she finally messaged Meera, saying, "I miss what we had. I'm grateful for all you were to me."

Meera responded, "moved and open to reconnecting".

That one shift—fueled by gratitude—helped Ananya regulate her emotional impulses, let go of blame, and rebuild a once-lost bond with maturity and grace.

Gratitude: The Inner Guide to Self-Control

Have you ever noticed how everything feels a little lighter when you pause and think about something you are truly thankful for?

That's gratitude in action—and it's more powerful than you might think. Gratitude helps improve *self-regulation* by changing the way we think and feel. *When we focus on what we're thankful for, our brain releases feel-good chemicals like dopamine and serotonin.* These chemicals help us feel calm and positive. This calm state makes it easier for us to think before we react. For example, if someone says something that upsets us, instead of shouting back or getting angry, we might pause and respond more calmly—because we've trained our mind to look at the bigger picture and not just react in the moment.

Practicing gratitude also helps us become more aware of our emotions. When we take time each day to think about what we're grateful for, we become more in touch with our feelings. This awareness helps us notice when we're getting upset, anxious, or angry, and gives us a chance to handle those emotions in a better way.

Over time, being thankful helps us build patience, reduce stress, and stay more balanced—even when things are hard. It teaches us to pause, reflect, and choose better actions. In simple words, gratitude acts like an inner guide, helping us stay calm, focused, and in control of our thoughts and actions.

Gratitude: Your Secret Weapon Against Stress

Now we know that each one of us faces stress. What is stress? In simple terms, stress is your body's reaction to various demands or challenges, both positive and negative, that can cause you to feel tense, worried, or overwhelmed. It's a natural response to things that require attention or action, and it can be triggered by a variety of factors.

Let's be honest—stress shows up in all our lives. Sometimes it's a big thing, like a tough exam or a fight with someone we care about. Other times, it's just a bunch of small things piling up—like being late, not sleeping well, or feeling like no one understands you. Sound familiar?

You may be surprised but yes, stress is necessary—*but only in the right amount*. This is called *"eustress"*, or positive stress. It helps you stay alert, energized, and focused. For example, stress before an exam or a presentation can push you to prepare better. It can boost performance, increase resilience, and even help with problem-solving.

Stress becomes a problem only when it's chronic or overwhelming, affecting sleep, mood, or health. But in healthy levels, stress is your body's way of preparing you to face challenges. It's like a built-in motivator that sharpens your thinking and gets you moving.

Now here's something you might not expect: gratitude—yes, just being thankful—can actually help you feel less stressed. You might wonder, "How can saying thanks or writing down a few good things change anything?" But it really can. In fact, it changes a lot.

When you pause to notice the good—like a smile from a stranger, someone who checked in on you, or even a quiet moment to breathe—your brain starts to calm down. Gratitude helps shift your focus from what's going wrong to what's still going right. And that shift matters. It helps your body relax, your heart slow down, and your mind find some peace.

Stress can manifest in various ways, including emotional, mental, physical and social reactions. Some common symptoms include headaches, fatigue, muscle tension, anxiety and irritability. Now after reading this I am not saying that you ignore the hard stuff. It just means you give your brain some breathing room—so you're not drowning in stress all the time.

When stress becomes too much, it's important to manage it before it affects your health and well-being. Here are various ways to overcome such challenges or roadblocks in life, especially when stress feels overwhelming: Practicing Gratitude, Breaking tasks into small steps, Practising Mindfulness and Meditation, Seek Support, Start Physical activity, Reframe Negative Thought, Create a routine and Focus on what you can control.

You would have noticed that the first tool advised is Practising Gratitude. It's all about focusing on what's going well and that shifts your mindset from *stress to appreciation*. A daily gratitude journal can calm anxiety and boost emotional resilience.

Also let's explore how gratitude can be a simple but powerful tool to handle stress better. We'll look at how it works, why it works, and how you can start using it today—even if life feels a little messy. Because sometimes, the smallest habit can create the biggest change.

The Final Pitch

Let's learn from Anaya, a 20-year-old college student, was chosen to present her startup idea at a national entrepreneurship competition. As the event neared, she felt the familiar knots in her stomach, her heart raced, and doubts crept in. "What if I mess up?" she thought.

But instead of panicking, she recognized this stress as a sign that she cared. She used the energy to sharpen her slides, practice her speech, and anticipate tough questions. The night before the pitch, she still felt nervous—but she was prepared.

On stage, the adrenaline helped her stay focused and alert. Her ideas flowed with clarity and confidence. The judges loved her presentation. Later, when asked how she stayed so composed, Anaya smiled and said, "I turned my stress into fuel."

Balancing the Books—and the Mind

Amit, 52, was a senior portfolio manager at a reputed financial firm. He had spent over two decades analyzing numbers, managing client portfolios, and leading teams. But lately, work had begun to feel like a battlefield.

The biggest source of his stress? His new boss—sharp, successful, but extremely demanding. He micromanaged everything, questioned every small decision, and constantly changed his expectations. One day, he'd praise a strategy. The next, he'd rip it apart. After every review meeting, Amit was left second-guessing himself, drained and confused.

He started losing sleep. Even weekends felt like extensions of work, with his mind replaying meetings or anticipating the next round of criticism. He found himself snapping at his team, withdrawing from colleagues, and feeling like a shadow of his former self.

Then one day, his company hosted a corporate wellness seminar focused on stress management. Amit had no interest in attending. But his colleague convinced him it might help, so he reluctantly joined.

The seminar was full of tips on relaxation and mental well-being, but one statement made a lasting impact: "Gratitude won't change the situation, but it can shift your perspective."

That night, half-heartedly, he jotted down three things he was grateful for:

- *A team member who backed him during a tense meeting*
- *His morning coffee ritual that gave him a quiet moment*
- *His decades of knowledge that no one could take away*

He kept at it. Every night, just a few lines. He made it a habit, noting down three things every evening. At first, it felt forced, but over time, the exercise started to shift his mindset. Amit found that when he focused on what he was grateful for, the pressure he felt at work became easier to handle. Instead of spiraling into stress after difficult meetings with his boss, Raj. He began to take a moment to pause and reflect on what was working. He appreciated the support of his colleagues, the sense of purpose he still felt in his work, and the growth he had achieved in his career.Over time, something shifted. Amit still had the same boss, but he didn't let the confusion paralyze him. Instead of reacting emotionally, he started focusing on what he could control. Gratitude grounded him. It felt like a lightbulb moment.

Amit had heard about gratitude before, but this idea—that it could be a tool to help him manage stress—had never clicked. The thought of using gratitude to handle his overwhelming work life seemed almost too simple to work. He acknowledged the stress, but also the support around him, the purpose in his work, and his ability to lead his team with patience.

Most importantly, gratitude helped him shift how he viewed his demanding boss. Instead of being overwhelmed by Raj's unpredictable behavior, Amit recognized that Raj's constant criticism was challenging him to sharpen his skills and grow. Gratitude didn't make Raj less demanding, but it helped Amit navigate his relationship with him in a more composed way. Amit began to feel empowered, not as a victim of Raj's whims, but as someone who could choose his response.He even began appreciating his boss—not for his unpredictability, but for unintentionally helping Amit grow thicker skin and clearer communication.

Amit didn't quit. Instead, he reconnected—with his team, his values, and the reason he entered finance in the first place. Gradually, Amit found himself looking forward to going to work again not because the stress had disappeared, but because he had learned to manage it with a sense of calm and perspective. Gratitude didn't remove the challenges, but it gave him the clarity and emotional resilience to handle them better. He knew he could still thrive, even in the chaos. Gratitude not only erased the chaos but it also gave him the calmness to rise above it.

Turn the Pressure into Power

Stress is like a pressure cooker—it can create something wonderful or make everything explode. What makes the difference is how we choose to handle the heat.

By now, you've seen that stress isn't the enemy. In fact, a little stress can boost focus, fuel growth, and help us stretch beyond our comfort zones. That's called positive stress—the kind that nudges us forward. But when stress lingers, builds up, and weighs us down, it turns into negative stress—which can affect our health, relationships, and peace of mind.

That's where gratitude becomes your *secret weapon*. It's not about ignoring the problems or sugar-coating reality. Gratitude shifts your focus—from what's wrong to what's working, from lack to abundance, and from helplessness to hope. As the stories showed, even in stressful environments, a grateful mindset helps anchor you, calm your racing thoughts, and bring clarity to your next step.

Here are a few practical ways to put this into action:

- Start or end your day by writing down 3 things you're grateful for.
- When you feel overwhelmed, pause and ask, "What's one small thing going right today?"
- Practice gratitude in conversations—appreciate someone out loud.
- Use gratitude as a mental reset before stressful meetings or situations.

Stress is part of life, but how you respond is where your power lies. Gratitude doesn't erase stress—it transforms how you carry it. It turns tension into awareness, chaos into calm, and pressure into progress. *The more you practice, the more natural it becomes.*

Summary:

- Emotions shape how we think, act, and connect—they're not problems, but helpful messengers.
- Ignoring emotions leads to stress; understanding them builds emotional strength and resilience.
- Gratitude helps regulate emotions by calming the mind, boosting mood, and shifting perspective.
- Real-life stories (Riya, Ananya, Anaya, Amit) show how gratitude transforms stress into strength and helps respond with clarity instead of reacting in anger or fear.

- Stress is natural and can be useful, but chronic stress harms well-being.
- Gratitude reduces stress by helping you focus on what's working, not just what's wrong.
- Simple gratitude practices—like journaling, pausing to reflect, or expressing thanks—build inner calm and resilience.
- In tough moments, gratitude turns pressure into progress and helps you stay grounded.

Part 2:

Rising with Gratitude – Elevating Your Life

Chapter 4

The Rise Framework – Growing Through Gratitude

"Gratitude doesn't just lift up the people you show it to. It lifts YOU up, too."

—Sara Quenzer

Now that we have taken the first important step—pausing, reflecting, and rewiring our inner world with gratitude it's time to take the second step. We've seen how even small moments of thankfulness can calm our mind, improve our emotional strength, and bring clarity in times of chaos. That was the foundation.

Now, it's time to rise.

This part of our journey is about going beyond the inner shifts and turning gratitude into a daily way of living and leading. It's where we can begin to elevate our relationships, our purpose, our career, and our personal growth through consistent, conscious practice.

Rising with gratitude is not about perfection or pretending everything is always fine. It's about facing real life—with it's messiness and miracles—with a mindset that helps us grow instead of shrink. Gratitude gives you the wings, but rising is our choice.

As you move forward, remember this: gratitude isn't just a feeling—*it's a way of showing up in the world.* And when we rise with it, we don't just feel better—we become better, more grounded, more resilient, and more open to life's possibilities.

Let's begin.

- The five pillars of 'Rise': Reflection, Intention, Strength, Expansion and Elevation
- How gratitude fuels growth and personal development
- The art of rising above adversity with a gratitude-centered mindset

Rise – Growing Through Gratitude

Gratitude is not just about saying "thank you"—it's a powerful force for transformation in every aspect of life. Similarly, growth is not limited to moving forward; it's about rising above—above fear, self-doubt, and limitations that hold us back. *There is a deep relationship between Gratitude and Growth.* When we choose gratitude as our foundation, we begin to rise beyond circumstances, past failures, and external expectations. Gratitude goes beyond appreciating what we get or recognizing what we have; it serves as a driving force for personal growth and meaningful transformation.

Imagine standing at the base of a mountain, looking up at the peak. That peak represents your highest potential—your dreams, goals, and the version of yourself you aspire to be. The journey to the top is filled with challenges: steep inclines, unexpected detours, and moments of exhaustion. But what if, instead of focusing on how far you still have to go, you paused to appreciate the strength in your legs, the beauty of the path, and the lessons learned with each step? This is the essence of gratitude—it shifts your perspective from lack to abundance, from struggle to progress, from limitation to possibility.

Gratitude doesn't eliminate obstacles, but it changes the way we perceive and respond to them. It transforms challenges into opportunities, setbacks into stepping stones, and ordinary moments into profound experiences of growth. While practicing gratitude one should not assume that the path forward will be cleared of all challenges. It will change the way you see those obstacles.

Gratitude helps us see things differently. Instead of getting upset when something goes wrong, it helps us look for the lesson. Like, "What can I learn from this?" or "How can this make me stronger?" It doesn't make problems disappear, but it helps us deal with them in a better way. What we do is start finding meaning in everyday things and see growth even in tough times. Gratitude reminds us that even when life feels hard, there's always something to appreciate—like the people who have supported us, the strength we didn't know we had, or the lesson we just learned. It's like finding a small light when everything feels dark.

Gratitude is more than just a feel-good emotion—*it is a catalyst for transformation*. When practiced intentionally, it acts as a transformative force that influences mindset, emotions, behaviors, physical health and longevity, spiritual growth & fulfillment and stronger relationships and helps in fostering resilience, enhances self-growth, and empowers individuals to rise beyond their limitations.

The Rise Framework is built on five core pillars: Reflection, Intention, Strength, Expansion, and Elevation, all of these help us elevate our lives through gratitude. These pillars serve as a road-map for personal development, helping individuals shift their mindset, embrace growth, and navigate challenges with confidence. These also help in rewiring the mind, embracing growth, and rising above challenges.

The Five Pillars of "Rise"

1. Reflection – Learning from the Past with Gratitude

Growth begins with *self-awareness.* Reflection is the pillar and practice of looking back—not with regret, but with gratitude for the lessons, experiences, and challenges that have shaped us. Instead of dwelling on what went wrong, gratitude allows us to reframe setbacks as stepping stones toward progress.

Key Practices:

- Gratitude journaling to recognize past experiences that shaped you. Reframing challenges as stepping stones rather than setbacks.
- Practicing self-compassion by appreciating your progress.
  - Journaling prompt: "What past challenge am I grateful for because it made me stronger?"
  - Example: Someone who faced financial struggles may reflect on how it taught them resourcefulness and resilience.

2. Intention – Directing Your Energy with Purposeful Gratitude.

Gratitude is most powerful when practiced with intention. Setting clear goals and intentions rooted in gratitude shifts your focus from external pressures to what truly matters. It helps you align actions with purpose and cultivate a life based on fulfillment rather than scarcity.

Key Practices:

- Setting gratitude-based goals instead of fear-driven ones.
- Using gratitude affirmations to grow while appreciating where you are.

- Practicing mindfulness to cultivate presence in daily life and using gratitude to strengthen relationships with colleagues and mentors
    - Journaling Prompt: What are three things you're grateful for in your job before setting career goals?
    - Example: Instead of feeling stuck in a job and focusing on what's missing, a person shifts their mindset by appreciating their current skills, experiences, and mentors. This gratitude fuels their motivation to seek promotions, enhance their skills, or transition to a more fulfilling role with confidence.

3. Strength – Building Resilience Through Gratitude

Gratitude makes us stronger inside. Instead of just seeing problems, it helps us notice chances to grow. When things get tough, gratitude helps us say, "What can I learn from this?" You stop feeling stuck and start feeling more hopeful. It teaches us that hard times don't last forever. We learn to handle stress better, bounce back quicker, and not give up easily. That's what real strength looks like.

Life comes with obstacles, but gratitude transforms struggles into growth opportunities.

When faced with adversity, those who practice gratitude tend to bounce back faster.

Life isn't always easy—there are ups and downs. But when you practice gratitude, tough times don't feel as heavy. Instead of just feeling stuck, you start to see what you can learn or how you can grow. People who are thankful often bounce back quicker because they focus on what's still good, even when things go wrong.

Key Practices:

- Finding gratitude in struggles to reframe obstacles as opportunities.
- Using gratitude to develop emotional resilience during difficult times.
- Expressing appreciation for personal strengths and the support of others.
- Finding gratitude during challenging times to reduce stress and anxiety
- Journaling prompt: Think of a difficult time in your life. What did you learn from it? How did it shape you into a stronger person?
- Example: Losing my job was terrifying, but it pushed me to develop new skills. I'm now in a role I love, and I'm grateful for the growth that came from the setback.
- Journaling prompt: What is something you are working on right now ? How can you appreciate yourself instead of just the end goal?
- Example: I'm training for a marathon. Instead of stressing over finishing, I'm grateful for every extra mile I can run, showing me how much stronger I've become.

4. Expansion – Embracing Growth with an Abundance Mindset

When you focus on gratitude, you stop thinking about what you don't have and start noticing all the good things you do have—like your talents, opportunities, and people who care about you. This mindset helps you grow in every aspect of life—from school, friendships, goals, and how you think. Instead of being afraid to try, you feel more confident about taking chances and learn new things. You start to see challenges as growth opportunities, not just problems. When you believe life is full of opportunities, you become more open to new ideas, big dreams, and exciting changes.

Key Practices:

- Shifting from Scarcity to Abundance Thinking
- Practicing Gratitude for Growth Opportunities
- Welcoming Change with a Positive Mindset
- Celebrating Others' Successes
- Taking Bold Actions Without Fear of Lack
- Building Strong, Supportive Relationships
- Committing to Lifelong Learning and Self-Improvement
- Practicing gratitude for challenges that push you out of your comfort zone:
  - Journaling prompt: "What opportunities or possibilities am I grateful for today?"
  - Example: Someone who is hesitant to start a new venture shifts their perspective from fear of failure to gratitude for the chance to learn something new.

5. Elevation – Rising Beyond Circumstances

True growth happens when you rise above negativity, setbacks, and self-doubt through gratitude. This final pillar focuses on cultivating daily gratitude rituals, practicing mindfulness, and fostering a mindset that naturally attracts positivity and success.

When you're grateful, problems become lessons, and tough times help you grow stronger.

This mindset helps you break free from limitations, embrace change, and move forward with confidence. When thankfulness becomes a part of your everyday life, you naturally elevate your thoughts, actions, and your feelings get better too. Real growth happens when you're thankful for where you are now while still working toward your dreams.

Key Practices:

- Cultivating a daily gratitude habit for long-term transformation.
- Expressing gratitude outwardly to strengthen relationships.
- Using gratitude as a tool to maintain joy and fulfillment.
  - Journaling prompt: "What's one small thing I can think or do today to feel more positive and grow?"
  - Example: A person who feels stuck in their routine might elevate their day by expressing gratitude for the small joys in life, shifting their perspective from monotony to appreciation.

The Essence of RISE Through Gratitude

By practicing these five pillars, gratitude becomes more than just a feeling—it becomes a way to redefine struggles, reframe success, and rise into your highest potential.

How Gratitude Fuels Growth and Personal Development

Gratitude is not just about appreciating what you have; it's about using that appreciation to *fuel your evolution*. When you cultivate gratitude, you train your brain to see opportunities instead of obstacles, to focus on solutions rather than problems, and to believe in abundance instead of scarcity. Over time, this mindset shift builds confidence, resilience, and motivation, allowing you to grow and elevate your life.

The Art of Rising Above Difficulties with a Gratitude-Centered Mindset

Challenges are inevitable, but how we respond to them determines our growth. A gratitude-centered mindset helps you rise above adversity by:

- Reframing difficulties as learning experiences rather than roadblocks.
- Finding silver linings in hardships to maintain hope and motivation.
- Focusing on progress instead of perfection, allowing for steady growth.
- Strengthening emotional resilience, making it easier to bounce back from setbacks.

By integrating gratitude into your daily life through reflection, intention, strength, expansion, and elevation, you can rewire your mind and rise— not just in small moments, but in lasting, transformative ways.

Summary:

- We start by pausing, reflecting, and rewiring our inner world with gratitude—this foundation calms the mind, builds emotional strength, and brings clarity during chaos.
- Now, it's time to rise: take gratitude beyond internal shifts and make it a daily practice that transforms relationships, purpose, career, and personal growth.
- Rising with gratitude means embracing life's messiness and miracles with a mindset focused on growth—not perfection.
- Gratitude is more than a feeling; it's a way of showing up in the world that helps us become more grounded, resilient, and open to possibilities.
- The Rise Framework is based on five pillars that guide personal transformation through gratitude:
  - Reflection – Learn from the past by reframing setbacks as growth opportunities.
  - Intention – Set purposeful goals grounded in gratitude to align actions with true values.

    - Strength – Build emotional resilience by finding lessons and hope in adversity.
    - Expansion – Adopt an abundance mindset by appreciating growth opportunities and welcoming change.
    - Elevation – Cultivate daily gratitude habits to rise above limitations and attract positivity.
- Gratitude does not remove challenges, but it changes how we perceive and respond to them—transforming obstacles into stepping stones.
- Practicing gratitude helps us find meaning and growth in everyday experiences, even during tough times.
- Gratitude is a catalyst for transformation that positively impacts mindset, emotions, behaviors, health, relationships, and spiritual growth.
- By practicing the five pillars consistently, gratitude becomes a way to redefine struggles, embrace growth, and rise to your highest potential.
- Rising with gratitude means developing a mindset that:
    - Reframes difficulties as learning experiences
    - Finds silver linings in hardships
    - Focuses on progress, not perfection.
    - Strengthens resilience to bounce back from setbacks.
- Integrating gratitude through Reflection, Intention, Strength, Expansion, and Elevation rewires the mind for lasting, transformative growth.

Chapter 5

Gratitude and Self-Worth

> ***"Gratitude turns what we have into enough."***
>
> \- Aesop

Could simply being thankful for who you are be the first step to finally feeling worthy?

The Hidden Link Between Gratitude and Self-Worth

At first glance, gratitude and self-worth may seem unrelated. After all, gratitude is about appreciating life, and self-worth is about how we see ourselves—right? But the two are deeply connected.

When we practice gratitude for who we are, rather than what we do or have, we begin to detach our self-worth from external validation. Instead of saying, "I am worthy because I accomplished this," we start saying, "I am worthy, period."

Gratitude helps us:

- Recognize our intrinsic value beyond external success.
- Appreciate our journey, including failures and struggles, as part of growth.

- Silence the inner critic by focusing on what is good and strong within us.

Imagine waking up every day and acknowledging yourself with gratitude instead of criticism. Instead of thinking, "I didn't do enough yesterday," you say, "I am grateful for the effort I put in, and I have another chance today."

Flipping the Script on Negative Self-Talk

One of the biggest obstacles to self-worth is negative self-talk. That little voice in our heads that says, "You're not good enough. You don't deserve happiness. You'll never be successful."

Gratitude is a direct antidote to this self-sabotage. Every time you catch yourself in negative self-talk, try replacing it with a gratitude statement:

- Instead of "I'm not smart enough," say, "I am grateful for my ability to learn and grow."
- Instead of "I keep failing," say, "I am grateful for these lessons that make me wiser."
- Instead of "I don't deserve happiness," say, "I am grateful for the love and joy I already have in my life."

At first, this might feel unnatural. But over time, just like strengthening a muscle, your mind learns to default to gratitude instead of self-doubt. And with that shift, your self-worth starts to flourish.

Raising Your Self-Worth Through Gratitude

Our self-perception is shaped by a lifetime of experiences, societal conditioning, and the beliefs we hold about ourselves.

The way we see ourselves is shaped by our past, what society tells us, and the beliefs we've picked up along the way. Many of us don't even realize we carry self-doubt, feel like we're not good enough, or fear we'll never be as good as someone else. We often judge our worth based on things like our success, money, relationships, or what others think of us. The world around us keeps sending the message that we're not enough... not smart enough, not attractive enough, not successful enough. A lot of this negative thinking comes from comparing ourselves to others, remembering our past mistakes, or believing the hurtful things we've heard or told ourselves.

This relentless comparison leaves us feeling inadequate, always chasing validation outside ourselves. But what if the key to self-worth isn't in achieving more, but in appreciating what already exists within us?

This is where gratitude becomes a powerful force in rewiring self-perception. Gratitude shifts the focus from what we lack to what we have, from self-criticism to self-appreciation. When we start acknowledging our own strengths, experiences, and even our imperfections with gratitude, our self-worth naturally grows. However, gratitude has the power to rewire these limiting beliefs and transform the way we see ourselves.

Gratitude isn't just about appreciating external blessings—it's also about embracing who we are, our journey, and our inherent worth. When we practice gratitude intentionally, we shift our mindset from self-judgment to self acceptance, from scarcity to abundance, and from insecurity to confidence.

Gratitude's Power to Lift Your Mind and Self-Image

Scientific research has shown that practicing gratitude consistently changes neural pathways in the brain. When we focus on gratitude, we engage the prefrontal cortex, the part of the brain responsible for decision-making, emotional regulation, and self-awareness. Over time, this shift strengthens positive thought patterns and reduces the brain's tendency to dwell on negativity.

Think of your brain like a path you walk on every day. If you keep thinking negative thoughts or doubting yourself, that path becomes deep and easy to follow. But gratitude is like building a new road in your mind—a better way that helps you feel kinder to yourself, stronger, and more peaceful inside.

The Power of Reframing with Gratitude

One of the most effective ways to change your self-perception is through reframing—the practice of consciously shifting how we interpret situations. Instead of seeing ourselves through a lens of limitation, gratitude helps us see the strengths, lessons, and growth in our experiences.

Example:

- Instead of thinking, “I am not successful,” reframe it as, “I am grateful for the progress I have made and the opportunities ahead.”
- Instead of “I always make mistakes,” say, “I am grateful for my ability to learn, grow, and improve.”
- Instead of “I don’t measure up to others,” affirm, “I am grateful for my unique journey and personal strengths.”

By changing the way we speak to ourselves, we reshape how we feel about ourselves.

Daily Gratitude Practices to Raise Your Self-Perception

Here are some simple yet powerful ways to integrate gratitude into your self perception:

1. Gratitude Mirror Exercise: Every morning, look in the mirror and say three things you are grateful for about yourself. (Example: "I am grateful for my kindness, my resilience, and my creativity.")
2. Gratitude Journaling: Write down one thing daily that you appreciate about yourself—not just what you do, but who you are.

3. Gratitude Reframes: Each time you catch yourself in self-criticism, pause and replace it with a gratitude-based thought.
4. Body Gratitude: Instead of focusing on flaws, thank your body for all it does for you—breathing, moving, all senses functioning well, and supporting you every day.
5. Reflect on Growth: Acknowledge past challenges and express gratitude for how they shaped you into a stronger person.

Overcoming Comparison and Self-Doubt Through Appreciation

In today's world, it's easy to feel like we're constantly falling behind. We scroll through social media and see others traveling to exotic places, celebrating big milestones, or achieving success that seems just out of reach. This constant exposure to others' highlights can make us question our own worth.

"Why am I not as successful?"

"Why don't I look like that?"

"Why does everyone else have it figured out?"

Comparison is a thief of joy, and self-doubt is it's partner in crime. The more we focus on what others have, the less we appreciate what we already do. But gratitude has the power to shift our perspective. It allows us to stop measuring ourselves against others and start recognizing our own value.

How Comparison and Self-Doubt Impact Self-Worth

When we compare ourselves to others, we are often looking at their best moments while being painfully aware of our worst struggles. This creates a false narrative that we are somehow "less than." Over time, this negative comparison erodes our self-worth, making us feel inadequate and undeserving.

Self-doubt creeps in when we believe that our achievements, appearance, or abilities don't measure up. But what if, instead of focusing on what we lack, we shifted our mindset to appreciate what we already have? This is where gratitude becomes a powerful tool for overcoming comparison and self-doubt.

How Gratitude Helps Break the Cycle of Comparison

Gratitude teaches us to focus on *abundance rather than scarcity.* When we actively appreciate what we have, we naturally feel less envious of others and more content with ourselves.

Here's how you can use gratitude to overcome comparison and self-doubt:

1. Shift from "Why Them?" to "I Am Grateful For..."

Instead of looking at someone else's success and feeling inadequate, practice appreciative reflection.

- If you see someone getting a promotion, instead of thinking "I'll never be that successful," say, "I am grateful for the skills and strengths I bring to my work."
- If you compare your appearance to someone else's, replace "I don't look as good as them" with "I am grateful for my body, which carries me through life every day."

By redirecting comparison into gratitude, you take control of your mindset and reinforce your own worth.

2. Keep a "Self-Appreciation Journal"

Each night, write down three things you appreciate about yourself. They don't have to be big achievements—just small moments that remind you of your worth.

Examples:

- "I am grateful for the kindness I showed a stranger today."
- "I appreciate my ability to keep going, even when things feel tough."
- "I'm thankful for my unique sense of humor that brings joy to others."

Over time, this habit trains your brain to seek out what is good within you instead of focusing on comparisons.

3. Reframe Social Media Exposure with Gratitude

Instead of mindlessly scrolling and feeling envious, use social media as a gratitude exercise.

- When you see someone's achievement, instead of feeling less than, say "I am grateful that success is possible for all of us, and I am on my own journey."
- When you see a beautiful vacation photo, instead of thinking "I wish I could travel like that," say "I am grateful for the places I have already explored and the experiences ahead."

By turning jealousy into appreciation, social media becomes a tool for inspiration rather than self-doubt.

4. Express Gratitude for Your Own Journey

Your life is uniquely yours. The struggles, setbacks, and triumphs you've experienced have shaped you into the person you are today. Take time to appreciate your journey instead of comparing it to someone else's.

- Write a letter to your past self, thanking them for the lessons and strength they have given you.
- Look back at old journal entries or photos and recognize how far you've come.

- Remind yourself: "I am grateful for my personal growth, even if my path looks different from others."

The practice of self-gratitude and self-compassion

We often hear about the importance of gratitude—appreciating our blessings, recognizing the kindness of others, and acknowledging the beauty around us. But what about gratitude toward ourselves? How often do we pause to appreciate who we are, the progress we've made, and the resilience we've shown?

For many, self-gratitude feels unfamiliar, even uncomfortable. We are quick to celebrate others but hesitate to acknowledge our own worth. We critique ourselves harshly for our mistakes but rarely thank ourselves for the lessons we've learned. Self-gratitude and self-compassion are essential in developing a strong sense of self-worth and rising with gratitude.

What is Self-Gratitude?

Self-gratitude is the practice of acknowledging, appreciating, and valuing yourself—your efforts, qualities, strengths, and even your imperfections. It's about recognizing that you are worthy of kindness, including from yourself.

Instead of saying, "I should have done better," self-gratitude says, "I did the best I could, and I appreciate myself for showing up."

Instead of focusing on what you lack, self-gratitude helps you focus on what you already have within you.

What is Self-Compassion?

Self-compassion is treating yourself with the same kindness and understanding that you would offer a friend. It involves three key elements:

1. Self-kindness – Being gentle with yourself instead of overly critical.
2. Common humanity – Recognizing that everyone struggles and makes mistakes.
3. Mindfulness – Accepting emotions without judgment rather than suppressing or exaggerating them.

While gratitude allows us to celebrate our strengths, self-compassion allows us to embrace our flaws and failures without shame.

Why Self-Gratitude and Self-Compassion Matter

Many people struggle with self-worth because they set unrealistic expectations for themselves. They believe they are only worthy if they achieve certain goals, look a certain way, or gain approval from others. This mindset leads to self-criticism, doubt, and the constant feeling of never being enough.

Practicing self-gratitude and self-compassion rewires the mind to see worthiness as inherent rather than something that must be earned. When you appreciate yourself, you:

- Develop inner confidence rather than seeking validation from others.
- Reduce self-criticism and increase self-acceptance.
- Cultivate a healthier, more positive relationship with yourself

How to Practice Self-Gratitude and Self-Compassion

1. Start a Self-Gratitude Journal

Each day, write down three things you appreciate about yourself. Examples:

- "I am grateful for my patience in handling challenges today."

- “I appreciate how I supported my friend when they needed me.”
- “I am thankful for my creativity and unique perspective.”

This practice trains your mind to recognize and celebrate your own worth.

2. Talk to Yourself Like a Friend

When you make a mistake, instead of thinking, “I’m such a failure,” ask: "If my best friend made this mistake, what would I say to them?"

Replace self-criticism with kindness and encouragement. Instead of “I’m not good enough,” say, “I am learning and growing, and that’s enough.”

3. Practice the “Hand on Heart” Method

When feeling overwhelmed, place your hand on your heart and take a deep breath. Say to yourself:

"I am doing my best. I am worthy of kindness. I am grateful for who I am."

This simple practice soothes the nervous system and reminds you to treat yourself with care.

4. Reflect on Your Growth

Look back at where you were five years ago. What challenges have you overcome? What lessons have you learned?

Gratitude isn’t just about appreciating the good moments—it’s about recognizing how far you’ve come and honoring your journey.

Summary

- Comparison and self-doubt will always exist, but we don't have to let them control our self-worth. By shifting our focus from what we lack to what we appreciate, we step into a mindset of abundance, confidence, and gratitude.
- Instead of asking, "Why am I not like them?", start asking, "What can I appreciate about myself today?" When gratitude becomes our habit, self-worth becomes our foundation.
- Gratitude isn't just about appreciating life—it's about appreciating yourself. When you recognize your own value with gratitude, you no longer seek worth from external sources. Instead, you stand in your own power, knowing that you are already enough.
- Your self-perception is in your hands. The more you practice gratitude, the more you train your mind to see your own worth. By embracing gratitude as a daily practice, we no longer wait for external validation to feel worthy. Instead, we recognize that our worth has been within us all along.
- Self-gratitude and self-compassion are acts of self-love. They remind us that our worth isn't based on perfection or achievements, but on the simple truth that we exist, grow, and contribute to the world in our own unique way.
- When we practice gratitude not just for the world around us but also for ourselves, we rise stronger, kinder, and more resilient.
- Start today. Take a deep breath and say: "I appreciate myself." Because you deserve it.

Chapter 6

Gratitude in Relationships – Elevating Connections

"Let us be grateful to people who make us happy; they are the charming gardeners who make our souls blossom."

– Marcel Proust

What if one simple habit could make your relationships deeper, stronger, and more joyful?

Relationships are the heart of our lives. Whether it's family, friends, a partner, or even colleagues, the connections we build shape our happiness. Relationships thrive on appreciation. When we express gratitude, we nurture warmth, trust, and deeper connections. But in our daily routines, we often overlook the little things—kind gestures, patience, or simply someone's presence in our life. We assume people know we appreciate them, but unspoken gratitude can fade, making relationships feel distant.

But often, we take the people in our lives for granted. We get busy, assume they'll always be there, or forget to express how much they mean to us. This is where gratitude can make all the difference.

When we practice gratitude in relationships, we focus on what's good rather than what's missing. Instead of noticing what someone didn't do, we appreciate what good they have done for us. Instead of expecting love, support, or kindness as a given, we acknowledge and cherish it.

How many times has this happened to you that when something goes wrong in a relationship we forget to remind ourselves of all the good that had happened in the same relation in the past? Surely there must have been some good things that would have happened due to which you are in that relationship for this long. To constantly remind ourselves of those good qualities of the other person will help you to be in good vibrations with the other person and help you to strengthen your relationship.

Gratitude is like sunshine for relationships—it helps them grow stronger. A simple "thank you" or noticing someone's effort can make a big difference. It makes the other person feel valued and brings happiness to both people. The more we show appreciation, the better and deeper our relationships become.

Giving is the beginning of receiving means that when we give to others, whether it's our time, kindness, help, or appreciation, we start a powerful cycle. When you help a friend, show support, or say thank you, you are not just giving something away. You are also opening the door for connection, trust, and love to grow.

Think about it like this: If you plant a seed, it doesn't just disappear. It grows into something bigger. In the same way, when you give from the heart, those actions often come back to you in unexpected ways. People remember kindness. They are more likely to return it, support you when you need it, and create a positive energy around you.

So giving is not about losing something. It is actually the start of gaining more—more friendship, respect, love, and happiness. That is how gratitude and giving go hand in hand.

How Gratitude Strengthens Relationships

Gratitude turns ordinary relationships into extraordinary ones. Start today – tell someone how much they mean to you.

Imagine two gardens. One is watered, nurtured, and cared for every day. The other is left to survive on it's own, receiving attention only when it looks withered. Which garden will bloom? The answer is obvious—the one that is tended to with love and care. Relationships are just like gardens—they need nourishment, and gratitude is one of the best ways to keep them thriving.

Too often, we get comfortable in our relationships and forget to appreciate the little things—a friend checking in on us, a spouse making coffee in the morning, or a parent always being there when needed. When gratitude is missing, relationships can feel dull and unfulfilling. But when we actively express appreciation, it strengthens our bonds, creating warmth, trust, and deeper connections.

It makes people feel valued. A simple "thank you" can brighten someone's day. Imagine how good it feels when someone appreciates your effort—whether it's making a meal, offering advice, or just being there. Gratitude strengthens bonds by showing others they matter.

It reduces conflicts. Many arguments start when people feel unappreciated. When gratitude becomes a habit, we stop focusing on small annoyances and start seeing the bigger picture—how much someone contributes to our life.

It creates deeper emotional connections. Expressing gratitude helps people open up, trust each other more, and build stronger relationships. A heartfelt "I'm grateful for you" can mean more than any expensive gift. A grateful heart creates a deeper emotional connection, making relationships stronger and more secure.

Simple Ways to Show Gratitude in Relationships

- Say "thank you" often, even for small things.
- Write a short note or text to express appreciation.
- Focus on what you love about a person instead of what they lack.
- Recall happy moments together and express your gratitude for them.

The Power of Gratitude in Strengthening Relationships

Gratitude is more than just saying "thank you." It is about recognizing and valuing the people in our lives and making them feel seen and appreciated. Expressing gratitude strengthens the emotional bonds in all types of relationships. It can make people feel more valued, appreciated, and supported, leading to happier and more fulfilling connections.

When Thank You Means I Love You

Let's see the story of Amit and Riya, a married couple. Amit was always busy with work, and over time, he stopped noticing the small things Riya did—packing his lunch, listening to his worries, or planning their weekend outings. Riya felt unappreciated and slowly stopped making these efforts. Their relationship began to feel routine, lacking warmth and connection.

One day, Amit read about the power of gratitude and decided to make a change. He started acknowledging Riya's efforts often, leaving her small notes of appreciation, and thanking her sincerely for everyday things. Slowly, Riya felt valued again, and in return, she also began expressing more gratitude towards Amit. Their bond got stronger, and their relationship felt happier and fulfilling.

This story is common—many relationships drift apart not because of big conflicts but due to a lack of appreciation. Gratitude acts as a glue that holds relationships together, reminding us to cherish the people in our lives instead of taking them for granted.

When you face difficult relationships or hurtful moments with someone, it is natural to blame the other person for what happened. But try this: blaming never helps you move past the situation, and it won't make things better. In fact, it often pulls you down further and makes things worse. You might wonder why you should do anything at all in this situation or why you would want to let goof the bad feelings toward the person you had a fight with. So read this:

"Holding on to your anger is like grasping a hot coal with the intent of throwing it at someone else; you are the one who gets burned."

- Gautam Buddha

To move out of this situation it's gratitude that will help you eliminate the uneasy feeling.

Use gratitude's magical power to transform your pain. Gratitude helps you to change this feeling into healing your wound. You may want to try this out.

Look for that relationship where the coal is still warm — where some connection remains, even if things have been painful. Offer gratitude to that person or relationship, and you may witness a magical shift in how you feel.

How can you do this? Take a moment to think back over your shared history. Remember the person's good qualities — the ways they helped you, supported you, or brought you joy. Recall the moments that made you smile or feel loved, before things changed or ended.

By focusing on the good, even in relationships that hurt, you allow healing to begin. Gratitude can soften pain, open your heart, and possibly transform the way you see the connection.

This exercise isn't about determining who was right or wrong, but is about healing yourself and the relationship. Once you complete this you will notice the restlessness settling in your mind and all the bad feelings will start to disappear. The reason we are doing this practice is also to improve our thoughts and energy and to get rid of any negative thoughts either related to any person or situation. When practiced over several days, you will realise that one day you have no more bad feelings towards that person.

You'll replace those hurting and negative thoughts with peace and happiness. The first evidence of gratitude's magical power working in your life is your feelings changing from negative to positive. In making your written list, make sure you do not forget to be grateful to the ones with whom you currently have good relations also. It is not all about improving our pained relations but it is also about strengthening our relations with our loved ones too.

Simple Ways to Show Gratitude in Relationships

1 Say "thank you" often. Even for small things—whether it's a home-cooked meal, a supportive conversation, a phone call or a thoughtful gesture from someone
2. Write a note of appreciation. A handwritten note, a text, or even a voice message can make someone feel valued.
3. Express gratitude for their presence, not just their actions. Let people know that their company alone brings you joy.
4. Do something thoughtful in return. Small surprises, acts of kindness, or simply spending quality time together can show your appreciation.
5. Maintain a gratitude journal for relationships. Write down one thing every day in your journal or diary that you appreciate about a loved one and take turns to write for each person you have in your life. A grateful heart creates a deeper emotional connection, making relationships stronger and more secure.

Benefits of Practicing Gratitude in Relationships

Apart from strengthening relationships, gratitude has many other benefits:

1. Brings more joy: Expressing gratitude increases happiness for both the giver and the receiver.
2. Reduces stress and resentment: When we focus on appreciation rather than complaints, relationships become more peaceful.
3. Encourages kindness and generosity: People who feel appreciated tend to reciprocate with more love and care.
4. Builds trust: A grateful heart creates a deeper emotional connection, making relationships stronger and more secure.

Expressing Gratitude Effectively in Professional Life

Imagine you are holding a small but powerful key. This key has the ability to unlock stronger relationships, boost happiness, and create a positive environment wherever you go. That key is gratitude—a simple yet life-changing habit that, when expressed effectively, can transform both personal and professional life.

Too often, we feel grateful in our hearts but forget to express it. We assume people know we appreciate them, but unspoken gratitude is like a wrapped gift never given—it holds value but never reaches the person who deserves it. Learning to express gratitude effectively can make relationships richer, workplaces more positive, and life more fulfilling.

The Power of Gratitude in Leadership

Indra Nooyi (former PepsiCo CEO) is well-known for her leadership style.One of her most touching leadership practices was writing thank you letters—not only to her employees but to their parents as well. When Indra Nooyi became CEO of PepsiCo, she wanted to show appreciation for her top executives in a way that went beyond the workplace. She realized that behind every great employee was a family that supported them. So, she started writing personal letters to the parents of her senior leaders, thanking them for raising such talented and dedicated individuals.

When employees' parents received these letters, many were deeply moved. Some even called their children, expressing pride and happiness. This simple act of gratitude strengthened employee loyalty and made them feel valued beyond their work roles.The letters made her employees feel appreciated and their families feel proud. This likely translated to higher workplace satisfaction, as feeling appreciated is one of the most significant factors contributing to an employee's view of their company.

Nooyi's story is a beautiful reminder that leadership isn't just about results—it's about people. A small gesture of gratitude and acknowledgment can have a powerful ripple effect, inspiring loyalty, motivation, and a deeper sense of connection.

"When you show appreciation, you don't just uplift one person—you uplift an entire network of people behind them."

Expressing Gratitude in Personal Life

A Thank You That Changed Everything

Ravi and Karan have been best friends since school. They shared everything—laughs, secrets, and even failures. But as they grew older, life got busier. Karan got a new job in another city, and their calls became less frequent. Ravi started feeling like their friendship was fading.

One day, while looking through old photos, Ravi felt a wave of gratitude. He remembered how Karan always stood by him—during exams, heartbreaks, and tough family times. On impulse,

Ravi sent Karan a simple message: "Hey, just wanted to say thank you for always being there. I may not say it enough, but I truly appreciate you."

Karan replied instantly: "Bro, that means a lot. I've missed our talks. Let's catch up soon."

That small message rekindled their bond. They started chatting more often and even planned a trip together.

Sometimes, we forget to express how much our friends mean to us. But a small "thank you" can reignite warmth, strengthen the connection, and remind both people of the value of true friendship.

Summary

- Thanking someone is like offering flowers to God—a pure, heartfelt gesture.
- Just as flowers symbolize love, respect, and devotion, saying "thank you" expresses appreciation and honors the goodness in others.
- Gratitude creates a sense of peace, connection, and warmth for both the giver and the receiver.
- Stories remind us that gratitude has a ripple effect, inspiring and uplifting those around us.
- A simple acknowledgment can build lasting bonds.
- In both work and life, appreciation isn't just polite—it's a powerful game-changer.

Chapter 7

Purpose, Passion, and Gratitude

"Gratitude makes sense of our past, brings peace for today, and creates a vision for tomorrow."

— Melody Beattie

What if the key to discovering your purpose isn't in doing more—but in noticing more? Gratitude doesn't just celebrate life—it reveals what makes it meaningful.

Life is most meaningful when we wake up with a sense of purpose and excitement. When we love what we do, when our days feel fulfilling, and when we connect deeply with what truly matters to us, life becomes joyful. But what if we don't always feel that way? What if we struggle to find purpose or lose our passion along the way? This is where gratitude plays a powerful role.

Gratitude is often seen as a way to appreciate what we have, but it is also a bridge to discovering our purpose and passion. It helps us focus on what brings us joy, what we are naturally drawn to, and what truly matters in our lives

Gratitude as a Compass for Purpose

Many people spend their lives searching for their true purpose, feeling lost or unsure of what they should be doing. But purpose isn't always something grand or world-changing—it is often found in the simple things that bring us happiness and meaning. Gratitude helps us recognize these moments.

Finding Purpose Through Thankfulness

Imagine two friends, Asha and Vikram. Asha spent years feeling unfulfilled at work, always chasing something bigger, never feeling satisfied. Vikram, on the other hand, started practicing gratitude. He began noticing what made him feel alive—helping others, teaching, and creating. Through gratitude, he realized that his purpose wasn't in climbing the corporate ladder but in mentoring young professionals. This shift in perspective changed his life.

By paying attention to what we are grateful for, we gain clues about our purpose. The things that light us up, make us feel excited, and bring us peace often hold the key to what we are meant to do.

Passion Grows with Gratitude

Passion is the fire that fuels our goals and dreams, but it can fade when we focus too much on what's missing rather than appreciating the journey. Gratitude keeps our passion alive by helping us celebrate progress, stay motivated, and find joy in the process instead of just the outcome.

For example, an artist who only focuses on selling paintings may lose passion when sales are slow. But if they practice gratitude—appreciating their talent, the joy of creating, and the ability to express themselves—they will continue to find fulfillment in their work. Gratitude shifts the focus from external validation to internal satisfaction.

Practicing gratitude doesn't mean we stop striving for success; it simply means we enjoy the journey while working toward our dreams. As we dive deeper into gratitude in the coming chapters, we'll explore how it shapes our relationships, careers, personal growth, and overall happiness. Gratitude isn't just about saying "thank you"—it's about seeing life through a lens of appreciation, which leads to a more purposeful and passionate existence.

How Gratitude Aligns with Your Passions and Life Purpose

Many people spend their lives searching for their true purpose—that one thing they are meant to do. Others seek passion, that fire within that makes life exciting and meaningful. But what if the answer isn't something we have to chase? What if it's something we uncover by simply appreciating the present? This is where gratitude becomes a powerful tool.

Gratitude isn't just about feeling thankful—it's about recognizing what truly brings us joy, meaning, and fulfillment. When we practice gratitude regularly, we start noticing patterns in what makes us happy, what energizes us, and what we feel deeply connected to. These clues help us align with our passions and life purpose.

Gratitude as a Guide to Passion

My story is a perfect example of this—after my graduation, I spent my first decade and a half in the banking & insurance industry. I always felt unsure about my career once I took a break from my work . I constantly compared myself to others, wondering if I was on the right path. But when I started keeping a gratitude journal, I noticed a pattern—that my happiness was always from moments when I helped people solve problems. Over time, this helped me to realize that my passion lay in coaching and mentoring, something I had never considered before.

By paying attention to what we are thankful for, we uncover the things that light us up from within. The more gratitude we practice, the more clarity we gain about what truly excites us. Gratitude shifts our focus from what we don't have to what we already possess. It helps us embrace our role, no matter how big or small, and find fulfillment in it.

Passion isn't always a sudden, dramatic realization—it's often hidden in the things we enjoy doing every day. When we practice gratitude, we begin to appreciate and acknowledge the activities, experiences, and moments that bring us true joy. When gratitude becomes a habit, passion follows naturally, and purpose becomes clearer. Instead of searching outside, gratitude helps us look within—and that's where our true calling has always been waiting.

Practical Exercises for Cultivating Purposeful Gratitude

Gratitude is a powerful tool that can help you discover your passion and life purpose. By shifting your focus from what's missing to what's already meaningful in your life, you gain clarity on what excites you, fulfills you, and aligns with your true self. Below are some practical exercises to help you cultivate purposeful gratitude and identify the connection between gratitude, passion, and purpose.

The Gratitude & Passion Journal

Objective: Identify patterns in what makes you feel truly alive.

How to Do It:

- Every day, write down three things you are grateful for.
- Reflect on which moments in your day brought you the most joy or energy.
- Over time, look for patterns—are you consistently grateful for helping others, being creative, solving problems, or teaching?
- These repeated moments of gratitude reveal your core passions and interests.

The Peak Gratitude Reflection

Objective: Discover when you have felt the most purposeful in life.

How to Do It:

- Think of three moments in your life when you felt deeply fulfilled, excited, or aligned with something meaningful.
- Write them down and express gratitude for those moments.
- Ask yourself: What was I doing? Who was I with? What impact did I have?
- The common themes in these experiences provide insights into what truly matters to you.

Summary

- Life feels meaningful when we wake up excited and understand why we do what we do.
- Finding purpose or passion can sometimes be challenging.
- Gratitude helps us by being more than just saying "thank you" — it guides us to discover what truly makes us happy.
- Paying attention to what we appreciate reveals clues about our purpose and what we love.
- Focusing on what we enjoy, rather than what's missing, helps passion grow.
- Gratitude keeps us motivated and joyful throughout the journey, not just at the destination.
- Practicing gratitude daily helps uncover our true passions and live with purpose and joy.
- Instead of searching outside, gratitude encourages us to look within, where our real calling awaits.

Chapter 8

Overcoming Challenges with Gratitude

"Be grateful for your difficulties and challenges, for they hold blessings. In fact... Man needs difficulties; they are necessary for health personal growth, individuation and self-actualisation."

- Carl Jung

Gratitude in Difficult Times: Reframing Setbacks

In the earlier chapters, we explored how gratitude brightens life—improving relationships, bringing peace, and helps us notice the good in everyday moments. We learned daily practices like writing in a journal, morning and evening rituals, and taking short gratitude pauses during the day. All of this helps us build a strong foundation—a mindset that naturally leans toward positivity.

But what about when life gets tough?

It is one thing to feel grateful when things are going well. When we are happy, healthy, and supported, gratitude flows easily. But what about those hard days? The moments when nothing seems to go right, when we feel hurt, disappointed, rejected, or lost?

That is where this chapter begins—because gratitude is not just for the good times. It can be a powerful light even in the darkest moments. In fact, that's when we need it the most.

Gratitude during difficult times is not about ignoring pain or pretending to be happy. It's about shifting how we look at the situation. It's choosing to see the whole picture—not just what is broken, but also what is still standing. Not just what we have lost, but what we have learned or gained along the way.

Let us take an example.

Imagine someone who loses a job. At first, it feels like failure, like rejection. It is scary and upsetting. But over time, this person might say, "That job loss gave me the push I needed to try something new. It helped me discover a better path." That does not mean the pain was not real—but through gratitude, they found meaning in the setback. They reframed it.

This process is called *reframing*, and it is one of the quiet powers of gratitude. It does not remove the challenge, but it helps us view it differently. We start to ask:

- What is this teaching me?
- What strength is growing in me through this?
- What or who am I still thankful for, even now?

These kinds of questions don't solve every problem, but they help us move through pain with more grace and less bitterness. They give us space to heal and grow instead of getting stuck.

You may think, "But some problems are too big for gratitude." And you are right— some pain runs deep. In those cases, gratitude does not fix everything, but it can sit beside the pain, offering comfort. Like a comforting friend who simply holds your hand and says, "You are not alone. There is still something good in you. You are still moving forward."

So as we move into this chapter, remember: you have already built a strong foundation with gratitude. You have practiced it during normal days. Now, let us explore how to carry it into the stormy days—when it is harder to find, but even more powerful when you do. This isn't about being cheerful all the time. It's about being hopeful—learning to reframe setbacks not as dead ends, but as redirections. Gratitude becomes the lens that helps us see not just what we have lost but what we are still becoming.

Using Gratitude to Navigate Change and Uncertainty

Instead of seeing challenges painful or negative, we begin looking at them as moments of growth, strength, or new beginnings. Gratitude helped us change how we view hard times. Now, let's go a step further.

Let us talk about how gratitude can guide us when life is uncertain, or when big changes shake up everything we thought was steady.

Change may feel scary. Whether moving to a new city, a job or career shift, a breakup, a health diagnosis, or even children leaving home—it often leaves us with questions like:

- What now?
- Why is this happening?
- What will happen next?

We humans like the feeling of being in control. This is because it keeps our mind in zones that are known to us. We enjoy routines, familiarity, and knowing what to expect. So when change or uncertainty shows up, it can feel like the ground has been pulled from under our feet. We start to feel out of control because we do not know what will happen next and it takes us away from our comfort zone. That is where gratitude steps in—not to fix everything, but to help us feel steady, even when the world around us is shifting. Gratitude makes us feel hopeful, comfortable and reassured that if we have come so far we will make it further too.

The Anchor in the Storm

Think of life as a boat journey. On calm days, we sail smoothly. But during storms— unexpected events, tough decisions, or emotional upsets—the boat rocks wildly. That is when you need an anchor.

Gratitude is that anchor. It does not stop the storm, but it keeps you from drifting too far off course.

Let's say someone has lost their job, and for that person, the future feels uncertain. At that moment,the mind may spiral into fear: "What will I do? How will I manage?" But if you pause and anchor yourself in gratitude, you might say: "I am thankful for the support of my family," or "I am grateful for the skills I have gained that I can use elsewhere."

These small thoughts do not make the problem disappear, but they calm the panic. They help you feel more grounded, more capable, and less lost.

Why Gratitude Helps During Uncertainty

Gratitude keeps your focus on what you still have, instead of what you might lose or what you have lost. When your world feels shaky, it reminds you of your strengths, your relationships, and your ability to adapt. It reminds you that not everything is changing. Some things—like your values, your heart, and your past experiences—are still with you.

Gratitude helps you trust the process, even if you do not know the outcome yet.

Ways to Practice Gratitude During Change

You do not need big steps. Even the smallest gratitude practices can bring peace during chaos. Here are a few simple things to try:

- Daily grounding: Each morning, ask yourself: What's one thing I can be grateful for right now?

- Comfort objects: This means taking a few moments each day or week to write down something you're grateful for—no matter how big or small—and placing it in a jar or recording it in a notebook. It could be something like "a warm cup of tea on a cold morning" or "a kind message from a friend." Over time, the jar fills up with these positive moments, and on days when you're feeling low, you can pull out a few notes to remind
- Grateful breathing: When you feel overwhelmed, pause, take a deep breath, and whisper something you are thankful for. This helps your body and mind settle.
- Reframing questions: Instead of "Why is this happening to me?" ask, "What could this teach me?" or "What part of me is growing through this?"

Change as a Hidden Gift

Most of us do not welcome change. But sometimes, it leads us to exactly where we are meant to be. The beauty is, we do not have to enjoy the change to be grateful for what it brings later.

Gratitude helps us stay hopeful in the waiting. It helps us see new paths, even when the old ones disappear. It teaches us that uncertainty does not have to mean fear—it can also mean possibility.

So as you face change—whether small or life-shifting—let gratitude walk with you. Let it be your steady hand, your soft voice, your inner light. Because even when life is unclear, gratitude helps you remember: you're not lost, you're just becoming.

A Cup of Tea and a New Beginning

Meera was 52 when life as she knew it suddenly changed. For over 25 years, she had been a homemaker. Her children had grown up and moved out, and her husband had recently retired. Their house, once noisy and full of activity, now echoed with silence.

On top of that, her husband was facing some health issues, and she felt overwhelmed. She had no clue what came next. The uncertainty of her future felt heavy.

"I didn't know what to do with myself," she shared later. "I used to feel needed, but suddenly I felt invisible. Useless. My days had no purpose."

At first, she spent hours scrolling through her phone, watching TV, or just sitting in bed. But one morning, something shifted. She made herself a cup of tea and went to sit on the balcony. The sun was rising, birds were chirping, and for the first time in weeks, she looked outside instead of just at her thoughts.

"I don't know why," she said, "but I felt this small whisper inside that said, 'This is still a beautiful life.'"

That day, she began a new habit—nothing big or fancy. Just five minutes with her tea every morning, writing one thing she was thankful for in a little notebook. Some days it was just, "The sun is warm." Other days it was, "I talked to my daughter today," or "My husband smiled at breakfast."

Slowly, something inside her started to shift.

She began noticing new things—how she still had strength, how much she enjoyed painting (a hobby she hadn't touched in 20 years), and how peaceful mornings felt when she wasn't rushing.

"Gratitude did not change my circumstances right away," Meera explained, "but it changed me. I started seeing this season of life not as an end, but as a chance to rediscover myself."

Now, Meera volunteers at a local library, teaches art to young kids on weekends, and even runs a small blog where she shares her thoughts on gratitude and finding joy after 50.

"I thought I was lost," she smiles, "but really, I was just beginning again."

Finding Your Cup of Tea Moment–Like Meera's quiet moment with her morning tea, each of us has small windows in our day where gratitude can gently enter—even when life feels uncertain or unclear.

Ask yourself:

- What simple moment in your day brings even a small sense of peace?
- Is there a habit—like having tea, walking, or watching the sky—that you can pair with a quick gratitude reflection?
- Can you notice one thing right now that hasn't changed, even if everything else feels different?

Set aside just five minutes. Grab a notebook, or open a note on your phone. Respond to the prompts below:

1. Today, I feel uncertain about…

   (Let your honest thoughts flow without judgment.)
2. But even in this uncertainty, I am grateful for…

   (List 1–3 things, big or small.)

You don't need to have it all figured out. Gratitude helps you stay present, even when the path ahead is still forming.

Summary :

- Gratitude won't erase difficulty, but it can give you the strength to face it with hope, resilience, and grace.
- No matter what you're going through, gratitude helps you see that life still holds light—and that even in the dark, you are not alone.

Part 3:

The Gratitude Rewiring Toolkit – Practical Applications

Chapter 9

Daily Gratitude Rituals for Lasting Change

Starting Small, Changing Big

Imagine a tiny seed that, when watered daily, grows into a mighty tree. Daily gratitude rituals work the same way. By taking just a few moments each day to focus on what you're thankful for, you gradually reshape your mindset, build inner strength, and create lasting positive changes in your life. It's simple, powerful, and a habit anyone can build.

To introduce the 5-Why Gratitude Method

Objective: Uncover the deeper reason behind what brings you joy.

How to Do It:

- Pick one thing you are grateful for (e.g., "I love writing").
- Ask yourself "Why do I love this?" and answer honestly.
- Repeat this question five times, each time digging deeper into your response. By the fifth "Why," you'll often discover a core value or purpose behind your passion.

Example:

1. I am grateful for writing.
2. Why? Because it helps me express myself.
3. Why? Because I enjoy sharing ideas and emotions.
4. Why? Because I like inspiring others through words.
5. Why? Because I want to help people see life in a positive way.

You will have more clarity as to why you like writing and your passion for writing, which may be connected to your purpose of spreading positivity and inspiration.

The Gratitude Letter to Your Future Self

Objective: Envision your ideal future and align gratitude with purpose.

How to Do It:

- Imagine yourself five years from now living your dream life.
- Write a letter to your future self expressing gratitude for everything you have accomplished.
- Be specific—describe your work, relationships, personal growth, and how gratitude played a role in getting you there.
- This exercise helps you align your goals with gratitude and gives you a clear vision of what you truly want.

Gratitude Acts of Service

Objective: Use gratitude to find purpose through giving.

How to Do It:

- Identify a way to express gratitude through action (volunteering, mentoring, helping a friend).

- Pay attention to how you feel during and after the experience.
- If serving others makes you feel fulfilled, it could be a clue that your purpose is connected to contribution and impact.

When practiced regularly, these exercises help you connect gratitude with your passion and life purpose. The more you appreciate what excites and fulfills you, the clearer your path becomes. Gratitude is not just about what we have—it's about recognizing what we are meant to do with it. Start today, and let gratitude guide you to a life of passion and purpose.

Creating Morning and Evening Gratitude Rituals

In the hustle and bustle of life, our minds often race ahead—chasing to-do lists, worrying about the future, or replaying the past. What if just a few minutes of your day could gently rewire your thoughts, uplift your mood, and help you see life in a more positive light? That's exactly what morning and evening gratitude rituals can do. They may seem simple, but over time, these daily habits create powerful and lasting change. Think of gratitude rituals like brushing your teeth. You do it daily, not just when your teeth are dirty, but to keep them healthy. Similarly, practicing gratitude each day keeps your mind healthy and your perspective bright, even during tough times.

They offer a gentle pause—like a deep breath for the soul. And when practiced in the quiet stillness of morning or the peaceful close of evening, gratitude becomes more than a feeling—it becomes a way of living.

Gratitude rituals don't require fancy tools or big blocks of time. They just need your presence, your heart, and a few minutes of reflection.

Morning Gratitude – Starting Your Day with a Positive Note

The way we start our day often sets the emotional tone for everything that follows. If we wake up feeling rushed or already stressed, we carry that tension with us. But starting the day with gratitude can act like a soft sunrise in the mind—it brightens your mood and opens your heart to possibilities. Imagine this: before picking up your phone or scrolling through messages, you sit quietly and ask yourself, "What am I grateful for this morning?" It might be the comfort of your blanket, the smell of fresh air, the sound of birds chirping, or just that you've opened your eyes to this new day.

This small morning moment is powerful. It gently trains your brain to scan for what's good, rather than what's missing.

You can try this:

- Keep a small "Gratitude Pad" beside your bed.
- Each morning, write three things you're thankful for.
- Include one thing you're looking forward to in the day—it brings a sense of hope.
- Say a simple thank you aloud or in your mind.

It could be anything from yesterday, today, or just something small that brings you joy.

It doesn't have to be big. It could be as simple as:

- "I'm grateful for a warm bed."
- "I'm thankful for a fresh start."
- "I am grateful for my body being healthy and my senses being functional."

When you start your day with gratitude, you are telling your brain to look for the good. This sets a hopeful and empowering tone for everything that follows. You become more present, less reactive, and more tuned in to moments that matter.

Doing this daily is like watering the seeds of positivity—you'll notice a lighter, more mindful version of yourself showing up throughout the day.

Evening Gratitude – Ending with Reflection and Peace

At the end of the day, our minds often replay what went wrong—mistakes, arguments, or what we didn't finish. Gratitude can gently shift the spotlight from what was missing to what was meaningful and what went right. Something that brought you joy. It helps you look at your day through a softer lens. You begin to see the small wins, the kindness of a stranger, the laughter you shared, or the lesson you learned.

Your evening gratitude ritual is like a soft landing before sleep. It helps your brain focus on peace, appreciation, and the small wins of the day. This reflective practice doesn't just help you sleep better—it helps you close the day with contentment, not complaint.

Try This:

Before bed, take a few minutes to mentally replay your day—but through the lens of gratitude. Ask yourself:

- What made me smile today?
- Who was kind to me?
- What are you thankful for?

You can write your answers in a journal or simply say them silently. Even one moment of gratitude can settle the mind and prepare you for restful sleep.

Why These Rituals Work

Our brains are naturally wired to notice problems—that's how humans have survived for centuries. But we can train our minds to also notice beauty, kindness, and joy. When you begin and end your day with gratitude, you create a mental rhythm that strengthens this positive lens. Doing this once feels nice. Doing it every day changes you. Gratitude rituals slowly rewire the brain, training it to focus on the good, even in ordinary or difficult moments. Over time, your perspective shifts—you don't ignore challenges, but you learn to notice joy alongside them.

Morning and evening rituals create a rhythm of awareness and appreciation. They sandwich your day with intention and peace. It's like giving yourself a quiet high-five for showing up and finding meaning, no matter how small. When practiced daily, these rituals rewire your thinking patterns. You don't just notice the good—you expect it, even in hard times. Your mornings begin with light, your nights end with peace, and the space in between feels more aligned.

Over time, gratitude becomes your default setting. You'll start to notice more reasons to be grateful throughout the day, even in ordinary or challenging moments. Morning and evening gratitude rituals are not just about being positive. They are about becoming more present, more connected, and more resilient. These tiny acts, done daily, become anchors for emotional strength and joy. Like the sun rising and setting, your gratitude can frame each day with light—no matter what is happening around you.

So tomorrow morning, before the rush begins, take a deep breath and ask yourself, "What am I grateful for?" And before you sleep, let your heart whisper, "Thank you." It's a small practice that makes a big difference.

The Instant Reset of a Troubled Mind - Pause for Gratitude for Happy Living

In today's world, life often feels like a constant race— assignments to be done, emails to check, deadlines to meet, errands to run, and problems to solve. We go from task to task, barely stopping to breathe, let alone to reflect. But what if just a few minutes could shift your entire feeling? That's the beauty of the five-minute gratitude pause—a small but powerful practice that can bring mindfulness, calm, and joy into the busiest of days.

Think of it like a tea break for your heart. You do not need a yoga mat or a quiet mountain top or a sun-deck bench to lie on —just five minutes, wherever you are, to pause and appreciate.

Life moves fast. From the moment we wake up, we often jump into work, chores, messages, or stress. We rush from one thing to another without stopping to take a breath. But what if you could take just two minutes to feel calmer, happier, and more present? That's what the 5-minute gratitude pause is all about.

It's a short break you give yourself during the day to stop and feel thankful for what's good in your life. This small habit can help you slow down, enjoy the moment, and feel better—no matter how busy or stressed you are.

The Five-Minute Gratitude Pause for mindful-living

It's a short, intentional break you take during the day to stop, breathe, and tune into what is going right instead of what is going wrong. It is about stepping away from autopilot and checking in with your inner world.

You can take this pause in the morning, during lunch, in between meetings, while sitting in traffic, or even while waiting for your coffee to brew. The idea is to shift your focus from rush to recognition—from doing to being.

How to Practice It

Here's a simple guide you can follow:

1. Stop and Breathe: Take a deep breath in, and slowly exhale. Let your shoulders relax. Let your mind settle.

2. Notice Your Surroundings:

   What's around you that brings comfort or beauty? What do you see, hear, or feel that's nice? Maybe sunlight on your skin, the sound of laughter, the coziness of your chair, or the fragrance of something pleasant.

3. Shift to Gratitude:

   Ask yourself, "What am I grateful for at this moment?" It could be something big like a supportive friend or something small like your favourite snack or the fact that you made it through a tough morning.

4. Feel It Fully:

   Don't just think of gratitude—feel it. Let it wash over you. Smile if it helps. Let that feeling fill your chest like a warm light.

5. Carry It Forward:

   Before returning to your day, carry that grateful feeling into your next activity. You'll notice how even ordinary tasks feel a little lighter.

Why It Works

This tiny pause creates a mental space where peace can slip in. It brings you back to the present moment and reminds you of what you have, instead of what's missing. This also helps your mind take a break from stress. It breaks the cycle of rush and reactivity and invites you into the present moment. Gratitude practiced in this way becomes a tool for mindful-living—where you're not just existing, but fully experiencing.

When you do this often, your brain gets better at noticing the good stuff. You feel less rushed, less angry, and more connected to the people and world around you. It is like cleaning your glasses—everything becomes clearer and more peaceful. Over time, the 5-minute gratitude pause builds new habits in your brain. You begin to naturally notice the good, even during difficult days and moments. You become more patient, kinder to yourself and others, and more connected to the world around you. You learn to see only good around you.

It is like tuning your internal radio to a more peaceful frequency—one where joy, calm, and meaning are easier to hear.

You don't need a big event or wait for something big to be grateful. You just need a moment. Gratitude is about noticing the little things—and the more you notice, the more joyful life feels. So next time you're stuck in traffic, sipping tea, or taking a break, give yourself this simple gift: stop for five minutes, breathe, and say thankyou. This 5-minute gratitude pause reminds you that in the middle of your messy, beautiful, unpredictable day, there is always something worth noticing. You also learn to express gratitude even when your days are full of joy, happiness and fun moments. There is always something worth appreciating.

Let gratitude gently bring you home to yourself.

Conclusion

Gratitude Transforms the Way You Live

"Gratitude doesn't wait for a perfect life; it creates one."

- Kinnari Sonchhatra

Let Gratitude Lead the Way

You've reached the end of this journey, but the real transformation begins now—with you.

Gratitude is not just a feel-good idea. Its a life-shifting habit backed by science. When we make thankfulness a regular part of our day, it doesn't just lift our mood; it actually changes how we function. Studies show that people who consistently focus on what they're thankful for sleep better, feel more connected in their relationships, bounce back faster from stress, and even enjoy better physical health. Researchers at the University of California discovered that the participants who kept a gratitude journal for just 10 weeks reported feeling 25% happier than those who didn't. Practicing gratitude helps rewire the brain to notice the good, reduces anxiety, and trains us to focus on what's going right—rather than what's missing.

But reading about gratitude and living it are two different things. I hope this book has not only informed you—but inspired you. You now have simple tools, reflections, and rituals that can change your mindset, relationships, and life. The only step left is to begin.

Start small. Say “thank you” with intention. Pause each day to reflect on what went well. Look for beauty in the ordinary. Express appreciation to someone who matters. These practices may seem simple, but they carry the power to elevate your everyday experiences.

Gratitude works best when it becomes a way of being—not just a habit, but a perspective.

The people who embrace gratitude are not necessarily the ones with the easiest lives. They’re the ones who choose to see light in every moment, meaning in every challenge, and growth in every experience.

If you’ve ever wondered when to start living with more joy, clarity, and purpose—this is your moment. Let gratitude guide you. Let it shape your decisions, heal your past, and light up your future.

Thank you for taking the time to read. Now, I invite you to bring these insights into your everyday life.

I would love to hear from you. If this book has touched your heart, sparked a shift, or offered you new insight into the power of gratitude, I invite you to share your thoughts with me. Whether you’ve tried the tools and practices and noticed changes in your life, or simply want to reflect on your journey, your voice matters. If you feel called to share your experiences, ask a question, seek guidance, or connect for any reason, I welcome the opportunity to hear from you. Gratitude grows through connection—and your story could inspire another soul.

You can write to me at : coachkinnari@gmail.com
Connect with me on:
Instagram: @coachkinnari

Let’s continue this journey heart to heart